GET

BUSINESS

FUNDED

GET YOUR BUSINESS FUNDED

CREATIVE METHODS

for Getting the Money You Need

STEVEN D. STRAUSS

WILEY

JOHN WILEY & SONS, INC.

Published by John Wiley & Sons, Inc., Hoboken, New Jersey.
Published simultaneously in Canada.

For general information on our other products and services or for technical support, please contact our Customer Care Department within the United States at (800) 762-2974, outside the United States at (317) 572-3993 or fax (317) 572-4002.

Wiley also publishes its books in a variety of electronic formats. Some content that appears in print may not be available in electronic books. For more information about Wiley products, visit our website at www.wiley.com.

Library of Congress Cataloging-in-Publication Data:

Strauss, Steven D., 1958–
   Get your business funded: creative methods for getting the money you need/Steven D. Strauss.
      p. cm.
   ISBN 978-0-470-92811-0 (pbk.); ISBN 978-1-118-08655-1 (ebk);
ISBN 978-1-118-08663-6 (ebk); ISBN 978-1-118-08665-0 (ebk)
   1. Small business—Finance.   2. Business enterprises—Finance.
   3. New business enterprises—Finance.   4. Venture capital.   I. Title.
   HG4027.7.S857 2011
   658.15'224—dc22

                                                                    2011002029

Printed in the United States of America
10 9 8 7 6 5 4 3 2 1

*This book is dedicated to all
of my great readers over the years.
You have allowed me to follow my dream.
Thank you so much.*

Contents

❧ SECTION IV: Creative Online Options

❧ SECTION V: Other Creative Options

❧ SECTION VI: In-Kind Contributions

Acknowledgments

I would like to thank Maria, Jillian, Sydney, Mara, Larry, and Spencer for their love and support. I would also like to thank my friends at John Wiley & Sons.

About the Author

Steve Strauss
Small Business
www.MrAllBiz.com

Steven D. Strauss, often called "America's leading small business expert," is an internationally recognized author, columnist, lawyer, and speaker. He is the senior business columnist for USATODAY.com and his column, "Ask an Expert," is one of the most highly syndicated business columns in the world. Steve is also the small business columnist for American Express OPEN Forum, and AT&T. He is the author of 15 books, including *The Small Business Bible*.

A highly sought-after commentator and media guest, Steve has been on ABC, CNN, CNBC, *The O'Reilly Factor*, and scores of other shows. He is a regular guest on both MSNBC's business show *Your Business* and *ABC News Now*. Steve is regularly seen in magazines and newspapers such as *Time, Inc., Entrepreneur, Success, New York*, the *Los Angeles Times*, the *Chicago Tribune*, the *New York Daily News*, and many more.

Steve often speaks to groups the world over, including a recent visit to the United Nations. He sits on the Board of the World Entrepreneurship Forum, and is also a speaker for the US State Department, speaking in places such as the West Bank, South Korea, Bahrain, Japan, Mongolia, and Jordan. He is often asked to be the small business spokesperson for companies that wish to reach the small business marketplace.

Steve is also an entrepreneur. He is president of The Strauss Group Inc., which includes the Strauss Law Firm, Strauss Seminar Co., Strauss Syndication, and MrAllBiz.com. He graduated from UCLA, the Claremont Graduate School, and the McGeorge School of Law, and was a Coro Foundation Fellow in Public Affairs. If you would like Steve to help you get *your* business funded, have him speak to your group, or to sign up for his free newsletter *Small Business Success Secrets!*, please visit his website, www.MrAllBiz.com.

Introduction

Getting the money to fund a business used to be easier.

Back in the day, options abounded. Banks had ready capital to lend, and if you did not qualify, Small Business Administration (SBA)-backed loans were available. If they didn't suit your needs, then you might have considered a home equity loan; with housing prices rising at near a 10 percent annual clip, entrepreneurs often tapped the home equity ATM. Low-doc or no-doc home equity loans were common, as were loans of 125 percent of the value of your residence. If you needed bigger bucks, venture capitalists and angel investors were more than happy to get you some cash in exchange for a piece of the pie.

Those days, as we all know too well, are long gone. The housing bubble burst. The mortgage crisis hit. The stock market tumbled. Capital markets dried up.

As a result, today, while many of those funding options are still around, terms and conditions, as they say, apply. There is less money and it is harder to get. But "harder" is not the same as "impossible." If having less money available is the bad news, the good news is that not only is it still available, but a crop of new, creative options have also emerged. You just have to know where to look.

This book is the right place to start.

As the senior business columnist for USATODAY.com, author of *The Small Business Bible,* and a popular speaker on the business lecture circuit, I get to meet a lot of entrepreneurs. What I know is that money is still out there; it's just hidden a little better these days. Finding the money you need to start, run, or grow your business today takes more creativity and, probably, a few more sources than you may anticipate. But it is still out there.

That's where I come in. In this book, you will find, and learn how to tap into, scores of ways to fund your business—everything from traditional bank and SBA loans to new and more novel ideas like crowd-funding and microfinance. The money is still out there, and I'll tell you where to find it.

"If I do my job right, yours just got easier."®

—Steve Strauss
www.MrAllBiz.com

Overview: Understanding the Funding Process

"Show me the money!" Cuba Gooding famously screamed to Tom Cruise in *Jerry Maguire*, but it just as easily could be said by many a small business person these days. There is no doubt that finding the money to start, run, or grow a business is more challenging today than in the recent past. But that said, it is still very doable.

Want proof? As you drive down the street, notice all of the small businesses that line the road. Or do a Google search for all of the small businesses in your city. There are *a lot* of small businesses—in your city, in your state, and in the country. How many? Try 30 million or so.

If they found the money, so can you.

In all likelihood, finding the money you need will require that you tap several resources, not just one or two, as had been the case previously. Let's say that you need $100,000 to start a business. While one loan for the whole amount is possible, what is far more probable is that you might instead use a combination of some of the following:

- Savings
- Retirement funds
- Credit cards
- Friends and family loans
- SBA loans
- Crowdfunding
- Microloans

Financing comes in a variety of forms and as such, if you want to fund your dream you too will need to be creative and resourceful.

WHAT WORKS?

Whatever sources you eventually use to fund your business, it will nevertheless be true that there are some things you can do to ensure that you get fully funded, and make no mistake about it—not having all the money you need seriously damages your ability to successfully execute your plans. Now, is it true that you may not get all the money you want, or when you want it? Of course. In fact, it is probably safe to say that a majority of startups begin with less than optimal funding. Yet even so, the following tips will assist you in getting as close to that magic 100 percent funded figure as possible.

(Note: This book is intended to offer a multitude of funding options for whatever needs a reader may have, be it starting a business, expanding, meeting payroll, or what have you. Accordingly, those options will generally be used interchangeably herein, unless circumstances require otherwise; i.e., a resource is more applicable to startups than growth.)

Understand the difference between debt and equity financing. Historically, there have been two ways to finance a business—debt financing and equity financing. (Note: Today, there are many more options available that don't fall so easily into these broad categories, for example, a new concept called crowdfunding. These too will be discussed thoroughly.)

Debt financing is, as the name suggests, where you take on debt to finance the business. This may be a bank or family loan, for instance, but whatever type it is, the distinguishing characteristic is that you take on debt that you must pay back.

Equity financing is different. Equity financing occurs when you barter away or sell a portion of your business in exchange for cash. This is money you do not have to pay back. The catch is that you end up owning less than 100 percent of the business and will have "partners" to consider.

Both debt and equity options are discussed throughout the book.

Draft a business plan. Maybe you think you do not need a business plan because you plan on completely financing your startup or growth endeavor on your own with no outside investors. Wrong. You still need a business plan.

Consider this: Would a pilot ever fly from New York to Los Angeles without a flight plan? Of course not. His flight plan tells him in which direction to head, how much fuel he will need, important landmarks to look for on the way, and so on. It lets him know whether he is headed in the right direction or is off-course.

Well, that is what your business plan is; it is your flight plan for success. It helps you understand whether you are headed in the right direction, what to look out for on the way, and whether you have the resources to get where you plan on going.

But beyond that, if you plan on getting any outside funding for your business, your potential investors will expect to see a well-drafted and well-thought-out business plan. (For a sample business plan, please see the Appendix.)

> Want help drafting your business plan? Here are two options: The Small Business Administration (SBA) offers free online business plan consulting. Their toolkit offers everything you need to complete an attractive business plan quickly. Also, Palo Alto Software makes a great business plan drafting program called Business Plan Pro. It will walk you through all the steps necessary to create a top-notch plan, like the one they provided in the Appendix to this book.

Value your business. Of course, if yours is a startup, there is no value to the business. But if you already have an ongoing concern, then before looking for funding, it is essential that you have a very clear idea about what your business is worth before seeking out the various funding sources. Let's say you are looking for $100,000. Would an equity partner receive 20 percent of your business for that investment, or 50 or 90 percent? You don't know without knowing what your business is worth.

To learn what your business is worth, you can:

- Pay for a business valuation. Google "Business valuation" and your city.
- Check out BizEquity.com. The simple, seven-step process on this site is a great tool.
- Check out my book, *The Small Business Bible*. There is a section on business valuation methods in there.

Have clear returns on investment. How will investors benefit from investing in your business? When should a bank expect to have its loan paid in full? You need to know the answers to questions like these before you seek funding.

Be patient. A word of warning: In business, the money game requires patience, period. In all likelihood, finding the money you require will take longer than you want or expect. It's sort of like a home improvement project—generally, they take longer (and cost more) than desired. This is a similar situation. This fact may require that you re-jigger your plans a bit, or execute them in stages instead of all at once. Alas, that is the nature of the funding game these days.

Patience is a virtue.

Be flexible. Flexibility looks all sorts of ways:

- You may have to be willing to pay a higher interest rate for the money you get.
- You might have to barter away a bigger chunk of the business than plans called for.
- Maybe you will need to start later, or smaller, than you anticipated.

Be frugal. It is always a good idea to keep your overhead low, but with money tighter than before it is all the more important. Because you will likely get your money in stages instead of all at once, you will probably need to make what money you do get last longer. Moreover, investors will want to see that you use your money wisely.

Frugality works all the way around.

Bottom Line: In the movie *The Edge*, characters played by Anthony Hopkins and Alec Baldwin are stranded in the Alaskan outback. With only a few tools and a small survival book, the pair seem destined for a cruel ending. But Hopkins studies the book carefully, and when a bear starts to stalk them, he finds a section on how to kill a bear. Baldwin is convinced they are doomed, no matter what the book says, but Hopkins tells him, "What one man can do another can do!" In the end, they kill the bear.

No, getting the money you need for your business may not be easy, but you too can kill your bear. What one man can do, another can do!

SECTION I

The Traditional Route

CHAPTER 1

Personal Assets

Essential Idea: Tap Your Own Personal Assets to Get the Money You Need

When my colleague Jim wanted to start his own business, it seemed out of reach. His credit was not the best. He did not have wealthy parents and so the friends and family plan seemed like a long shot. And he had little in actual savings, so even that was not a viable option.

But Jim got creative and found a way to launch his dream. Today he is four years self-employed, happy, and making a good living. How did he do it?

- Although he did not have any savings, he did have some stocks that he had held on to through the years. Though he liked owning them, he liked the idea of owning his own business more. He sold his shares.
- Even though he did not have wealthy parents, he did have a grand-father who was likely going to give him a small inheritance one day. Jim approached Gramps, explained the situation, showed him a simple business plan, and found that Gramps was happy to give Jim the money while he (Gramps) was still alive.
- And even though Jim had no savings, he did have a strong work ethic. Jim got a second job for six months, saved the money, and then used it to start the business.

Jim did it all without going into debt and without having to barter away part of his business. He did it by using his own resources. If Jim did it, so can you.

USING PERSONAL ASSETS

According to SBA.gov, "The primary source of capital for most new businesses comes from savings and other personal resources." Personal resources can mean all sorts of things: savings, money market accounts, stocks and bonds, whole life insurance, and more. Whatever the case, using your own personal assets is the subject of the first chapter of this book because that is where most people start when looking to fund a business, and likely where you will need to begin as well.

In addition, it will be very hard to ask anyone to invest in your business—be it a bank, angel investor, uncle, or whoever—if you do not have some of your own money invested too. Entrepreneurship is a risk. For you it is a risk of many shades: financial of course, but also emotional and professional. But lenders and investors have little interest in those latter two risks. What they want is to see that you are willing to accept your fair share of the financial risk. That is where using your own actual capital, like savings, also comes into play. For starters, it proves you are serious.

There are both pros and cons to this strategy:

Pros
- You incur no debt.
- It comes interest free.
- You need no one's approval.
- You will not be liable to others.

The last point is significant. The fact that you can get creative and possibly obtain some or all of the money you seek with no strings attached is no small matter. As you will see throughout this book, getting the money you need almost always requires the assistance and/or approval of someone else—a lender or an investor, for instance. But by using your own assets, you avoid that complication altogether. And not only do you not need their approval to use your own money, but you also do not have to pay it back to anyone else. Sweet.

One other benefit of having your own skin in the game is that you will likely be just that much more invested and committed to the venture's success. Of course you want to succeed and you plan on doing so, and while no one ever wants to lose someone else's money in a business enterprise, the fact is *it still is someone else's money*. Using your own money is like Cortez burning his own ships; it eliminates failure as an option.

> When explorer Hernando Cortez landed in Mexico, he wanted to be sure that his mission would be successful. Therefore, upon arrival Cortez famously told his men, "Burn the ships." His crew thought he was nuts, but Cortez repeated the command: "Burn the ships," adding, "If we are going home, we are going home in their ships." His men eventually acceded to the captain's order and did in fact burn their own ships. Why? Cortez had convinced them that by burning the ships, failure was not an option. By using your personal assets, you are burning the ships.

Cons
- You will in fact be using up your own resources.
- You may also be using your rainy day fund.
- It is risky.
- You still may not have enough to get started, and then what?
- It may not be the best use of your money.

That last point is significant. Starting a business is a big deal. The business will likely require a substantial infusion of capital to get up and running, and then stay running. As such, the question to consider is the potential lost opportunities of using your financial assets in this manner. Will there be other things that you will be unable to do or invest in because your money is tied up in your business? The answer is yes. You need to be comfortable with that fact going forward. Think it through carefully.

With those caveats in place, let's examine a little more closely the different ways to tap your different assets.

SAVINGS

The best way to use savings for a business is, to the extent possible, plan for it. That is, plan ahead and begin to save now for the money you will need later. Of course, you may not be able to save everything you need, but every little bit helps. It also may be true that you don't have time to plan ahead and you need the money for your business *now*. That is fine too. Not ideal, but fine nonetheless.

The other thing to consider when using a savings account is the extent to which this money is your safety net. Again, be thoughtful. Be a businessperson and analyze the pros and cons carefully. Sure, it is exciting and fun to start a new business, but it is depressing and terrifying to not have any savings in the bank. Double-check your plan and willingness to take a risk. In fact, you may want to even consider not using all of your savings for your business venture and instead keeping, say, $5,000 or so in the bank. That rainy day fund will likely come in handy someday.

INVESTMENTS

When people think of using their own money for their business, often "savings" are both what they consider and what they consider to be the stumbling block. Either they do not have enough saved up to make a difference or they are afraid of spending their nest egg. While the former is certainly understandable, the latter is less so in this context. If you want to start a business, the drive must be so strong that even your own bank account cannot get in your way. If it does, if the risk is too much, that is understandable, but can also be a sign that entrepreneurship may not be for you.

That said, it is important to understand that there is more than one way to skin a cat. People have all sorts of assets, not just savings. Mutual funds, stocks, bonds, CDs, pieces of art, antiques, old cars, new cars, baseball cards—all can be liquidated to serve your needs.

And of course there are all sorts of ways and places to sell your assets: an estate sale, Craigslist, eBay, a consignment store, the newspaper, and specialty newspapers and magazines, to name a few.

INHERITANCE

There are two ways to use an inheritance for a business.

The first is the inheritance that you have not received yet; that is, an inheritance you expect to get. You may be sure that you are going to get that inheritance, but truly, a person can change a will or trust at almost any time before their death. As such, this first method actually deals with the expectation of an inheritance.

Do you really want to ask your grandfather (for example) for an advance on that expected inheritance? That is the question you must ask yourself. If the answer is yes, then you begin this process by having a chat with the person from whom you expect to get the inheritance. Needless to say, this can be a very tricky, touchy, verging on tacky discussion, so first and foremost it must be handled delicately.

The important thing is to make the giver understand that it is a smart move on their part. There are two ways to do this:

1. First, explain how you see the money being used in your business and how it is a good use of the potential gift. This is where a business plan will come in handy. Although Gramps will likely never read it, he will feel better knowing it is there.

2. Second, explain that there are tax considerations involved. Currently, the tax code allows someone to give a gift of $13,000 ($26,000 if it is to you and a spouse) tax free. If the amount you want is more than that, the giver and you will need to consult with an estate lawyer so as to determine how best to make the gift. By treating this issue with the respect it deserves, you make your request for an advance on an inheritance more plausible.

The other thing to consider is the effect of the advance on the overall estate of the giver, and on the other people who will be sharing that estate when your loved one passes away. They may not like it, and may think that you are devaluing the overall estate by taking money out early. That is an issue you will need to handle.

The bottom line is that you need to be considerate of everyone involved, and equally professional. It may be a good idea to first speak with an estate lawyer and a financial planner. Learning how an inheritance advance may affect everyone else is important. Equally important is gently helping them to understand how it can affect you in a positive way by funding your dream.

The other way to use an inheritance for a business is the situation where you are actually already due money from an estate. This usually occurs in one of two ways:

1. Someone died and the estate is in probate. Probate can easily last a year, so in this scenario you may be due money but not for a while.
2. A trust was set up and has not been 100 percent dispersed.

> An inheritance can be created in many ways. The first is where the decedent died with a will and named you in that will. A second way is if someone died without a will but you are a close relative, an heir, and so you are due an inheritance as a matter of law. Third, someone can create a trust that takes effect either while they are still alive, upon their death, or upon the death of their spouse. Finally, you may be named as beneficiary of a life insurance policy, creating even one more sort of inheritance.

If this is your situation, what you can do is sell your right to receive the future money. If you did that, you would receive a smaller lump sum payment now. In the law, this is called "assigning" your rights. An assignment is a full and complete transfer of rights to someone else. As such, the first thing you must do is research if you can assign your rights to the inheritance in question. Not all inheritances can be assigned. This will require the assistance of a wills and trusts or probate lawyer.

The other popular option is to get a loan against the inheritance; the inheritance acts as collateral for the loan. The good news is that because there is collateral to secure a loan, practically anyone legally due an inheritance can get one, despite their credit score. Just don't expect to get very favorable terms.

Once you know that you can in fact assign (or get a loan against) your inheritance, then it is a matter of finding the right company and the best deal. Try Googling the name of your city and "probate advance," "inheritance advance," or "trust advance." Make sure this is a reputable company. Do your homework. Check them out on Yelp.com and get some references. Speak with a lawyer.

LIFE INSURANCE OPTIONS

If you have a whole life insurance policy, another option is to cash it in. The very nature of a whole life policy is that it grows in cash value the longer you own it and make premium payments on it.

Is this the right choice for you? That is a difficult decision. For most people who have children, life insurance is a critical component of being a responsible parent. It is also a vital component of a sound financial plan. Should something happen to you before you have earned enough to take care of your kids via your estate alone, life insurance is there to, well, insure that they are taken care of. Cashing in a whole life policy to fund what could be a risky business venture is, therefore, not often the best choice.

With that caveat in mind, here is how you do it, if you decide to:

- Call the insurance carrier. Find out what the cash value of the policy is and request the appropriate form.
- Fill out the form. You will likely have to have it notarized, so do that and send it back in. Your spouse may have to sign it as well.
- Get your check. It will probably take a few weeks.

One last, important note: As opposed to a whole life policy, it is very affordable to get a term life insurance policy. If you cash out your whole life policy, seriously consider replacing it with a term policy.

OTHER OPTIONS

Other popular options for using your own assets to fund a business include home equity loans and tapping retirement accounts. As these are more complicated procedures, they are dealt with in separate chapters.

Bottom Line: There are a lot of individual ways to invest in your business and you will need to use them, especially if you expect others to invest in you too.

CHAPTER 2

Bank Loans

Essential Idea: Get a Basic Business Loan from a Bank

If you want to understand how valuable—and critical—a traditional bank loan can be in the process of starting and growing a business, just consider the case of my colleague, Jeremy. Jeremy is a very successful airline pilot who travels all over the world. While he loved his job, Jeremy also wanted to start a real estate business on the side to augment both his income and his retirement.

To do that, he needed the help of a bank.

So Jeremy went to work. He met with some investment real estate agents and together they drafted a plan: Jeremy was first going to buy a small duplex, and over time, with the assistance of his bank and tax code laws that would allow him to sell the property and move up while deferring taxes (called 1099 exchanges), Jeremy would grow his real estate holdings. The bank liked the plan and the duplex, and they believed in him. So he got his first loan—and the plan was put into play.

It worked, big time.

After a few years, Jeremy sold that duplex and bought a four-plex. Five years later, he sold that, got another bank loan, and bought a small apartment building. I just heard that last week, Jeremy bought two more buildings (not selling any this time), worth more than $1.1 million.

All with the help of his bank.

OVERVIEW

The first place people usually think of when they want to get outside funding for their business is a bank, and that makes sense. Banks are in the business of lending money, they are good at it, and commercial lending is a bank's bread and butter. Banks especially like business clients because, as opposed to personal loans, business loans are typically larger and the risk is usually smaller.

Your ability to get a commercial loan from a bank depends upon many factors, but the first to consider is this: Do you need the money to start a new business or to run and/or grow an already existing business? The tough news is that traditional bank loans are much more difficult to obtain for a new startup than a more mature business (not impossible, just tougher).

Why is that?

It makes sense if you think about it. Banks are in the business of lending money, yes, but they are also in the business of making safe loans that have a high likelihood of getting repaid on time, and that make them money. But of all the loans a bank could make—to an established business, for a mortgage, for inventory, and so forth—loaning money to a new startup is probably the most risky. Consider the following:

- Startups have no business track record from which to base a lending decision.
- Startups have no sales track record so as to calculate profitability.
- Startups typically have few items with which to collateralize a loan.

So that is the general rule: startups don't get a lot of regular bank loans. But the good news is that the general rule is not the only rule. The point of this book is to help you get funded no matter the circumstances, and as you will see in this chapter and the next, there definitely are ways to get a bank loan, even for that new startup.

> Commercial lending is the lending of money or credit to a business for business purposes. Business owners like commercial loans because they help to establish (or expand) business credit. Institutions that engage in commercial lending include private banks, savings and loans, credit unions, financial groups, commercial banks, and hard money lenders.

But whatever the case—whether you will need funds for a new startup or you are looking for a loan for an already established business—the essentials of obtaining a business bank loan are the same, so read on.

LOAN BASICS

Getting a business loan will require that you jump through several hoops—properly and in order. You will need to have a lot of documentation prepared for the bank, and the bank will additionally look at your personal credit history, ability to collateralize the loan, business history, books (profit and loss [P&L] statements, balance sheets, etc.), and more.

Because an element of risk is involved in every loan a bank makes, your job is to make the bank understand that your loan's risk is low. You can do that better if you understand the "Four Cs" of credit. When a banker considers a business loan, it will analyze your application through this filter:

- *Character.* This factor relates to the integrity, reputation, and history of the borrower. In smaller community credit unions and banks, character is a significant factor, whereas in many big banks, your credit score matters more. Character is determined by your payment history, credit profile, letters of reference, and so on.
- *Capital.* How much money do you need? The more money you seek, the tougher it will be to get.
- *Capacity.* What is your ability to repay the loan? You will need to be able to show the lender that you will be able to service the loan amount requested and that it will be repaid in full and on time. Therefore, requesting too much is not a good idea.
- *Collateral.* Not all business bank loans require collateral—in fact, some are unsecured—but that is more the exception than the rule. Bankers like collateral. There are all sorts of options you can use to secure a loan: a home or other real estate, inventory, machinery, even accounts receivable.

So, if you need money, think like a banker and understand these four concepts before you apply.

THE APPLICATION PROCESS

Each bank has its own loan process, of course, but generally the application process can be divided into four steps:

1. Speaking with a bank officer in order to make a good first impression, and learning about loan options and eligibility requirements.
2. Filling out the application and providing all requested documents.
3. Waiting—for the bank to verify the documents, for it to analyze your credit, for underwriting, and so on.
4. Disbursement of funds.

The length of time it takes to gain approval necessarily depends upon the circumstances, size of the loan, type of loan, and the bank. It can be as short as a few days or as long as a few months. Somewhere in the middle is usually about right.

> Lenders offer all sorts of business loans. These are the most common: startup loans, business growth financing, loans for inventory, vehicle financing, loans for equipment and tools, property loans, and trade financing.

Maybe you are wondering whether there is anything you can do as you begin this process to increase your chances of getting approved. The answer is yes. These things help:

- *Cleaning up your personal and business credit reports.* If you have outstanding debts, get them current. If there are mistakes on the reports, get them corrected.
- *Having a good business track record.* If your business has a history of being solvent and profitable, that of course is helpful. If not, handle business now.
- *Having a good payment history.* Showing the bank that your business pays its bills in full and on time helps a lot.
- *Having a good loan track record.* The best thing of all is a history of borrowing and paying back loans in full and on time. If your business

has no such history, your own personal history, with a mortgage for instance, can be used.

- *Showing cash flow and profitability.* It's all about your ability to repay the loan, and profits make that possible.
- *Having collateral.* For example, real estate, automobiles, stock, vehicles, and cash.
- *Highlighting your experience.* Again, startups are different. If that is what you are seeking funding for, do not diminish the importance of your ability to show the lender that you are experienced at business generally and have successfully executed plans previously. If you can show that you are experienced specifically in the sort of business that is being proposed, all the better.

In addition to the aforementioned, if you really want to increase the chances of your loan getting approved, here is another suggestion: before you apply for the loan, prepare your own, additional loan package to present to the bank. Some of this information will be required by the bank anyway, but putting a whole package together cannot help but impress.

Your loan proposal package should include the following:

General Information
- Business name, address, URL, and all other relevant information.
- The management team, their contact information, Social Security numbers, and business background.
- Business description and history.
- Legal documents: business licenses, Articles of Incorporation, copies of any contracts you may have, and leases.
- Amount and purpose of the loan.

Business Information
- Your business plan.
- Your marketing plan.
- Your customers and sales record.

Financial Information
- Bank statements, profit and loss statements, balance sheets, cash flow statements, and other relevant financial records for the past

three years. If yours is a startup, then add in your projected financials.

- Accounts receivable and accounts payable.
- Business and personal tax returns.
- Personal financial statements and credit reports for the owners and management team.
- Dun & Bradstreet credit information.
- Collateral options.

The point of all of this information is to make the lender's job as easy and risk-free as possible. Therefore it is your job to present your business in the best light possible, but also authentically. Wildly inflated sales projections, for instance, can be spotted a mile away and really hurt your chances, so avoid that.

In addition, since not every borrower will be an AAA credit risk, there are other things that matter too. Sure, your numbers and history are important, but a good presentation is equally necessary. Present yourself and your business in a way that would impress a banker. Be professional. Be prepared. Be enthusiastic. And remember, bankers are a fairly conservative lot, so keep that in mind. Dress for success. Even if you are starting a surf shop, sandals and flip-flops are not a good idea.

> The Fair Credit Reporting Act (FCRA) requires each of the nation's three consumer credit reporting companies—Equifax, Experian, and TransUnion—to provide you with a free copy of your credit report, at your request, once a year. To order, visit annualcreditreport.com or call 1-877-322-8228. Do not contact the three reporting companies individually—they provide the free annual credit reports only through annualcreditreport.com.

INCREASING YOUR CHANCES OF GETTING FUNDED

As stated, business loans are not easy to get these days and it may be that you even need some extra help getting approved. Maybe you are new to business and have no track record or maybe your personal credit isn't the best . . . whatever the case, here are some final ideas:

Get a co-signer. A co-signer, as you know, is a person who chooses to sign on a loan in addition to the original borrowers. The purpose of a co-signer is to have an additional person with good credit on the application and willing to be responsible for repayment. By co-signing, the co-signer is agreeing to also be personally liable on the loan. He or she is as equally responsible for the debt as the other borrowers—not more, not less. Co-signing means that the debt will be reported to the co-signer's credit report and will go against his or her debt-to-income ratio. The debt's repayment history (for good or ill) will also be reported to the co-signer's credit report. If the debt is not paid back by the business or other borrowers, the co-signer will be liable for the debt.

In the case where a borrower must personally guarantee a loan (not uncommon in a business loan situation), having a co-signer can also make a big difference.

Needless to say, co-signing is a tremendous responsibility and should not be undertaken or requested lightly. Business is a risk, and not every risk pans out. So, while you may have someone close to you willing to co-sign, be aware that should the worst-case scenario ensue (and the worst-case scenario does ensue sometimes) the co-signer will be in a very bad spot. Co-signing for a loan has ended relationships. With that caveat in place, if you both are willing to take that risk, then congratulations—you may have just found a way to get your business funded.

> Before agreeing to co-sign a loan, the co-signer needs to understand the risks and benefits. The benefits to the co-signer are few, and mainly it will be in assisting someone they love (typically) to get their dream funded. The risks are numerous and as such, the decision should be a level-headed, business one. The co-signer should understand what the business is, how soon it stands to be profitable, and whether the owner can service the loan in question. Helping someone get a loan they cannot afford is not really helping them.

Talk to a pro. Studies indicate that speaking with a loan specialist or a financial counselor before applying for a loan increases your chance of getting approved. There are several places you could go for that, and most are free.

- The SBA has field offices in every state (SBA.gov).
- SBA Small Business Development Centers (SBDCs) have about 900 offices associated with various colleges and universities: Google SBDC and your city.
- The SBA also runs about 100 Women's Business Ownership Centers. Google that as well.
- SCORE is a nationwide volunteer organization where individuals with business expertise and experience give their time and knowledge to entrepreneurs, small businesses, and others. It is a great organization. SCORE offers free, confidential counseling both online and at SCORE offices (SCORE.org).

Work with a community bank. The savvy businessperson will look at both big banks as well when seeking funding for their business. Both are important in this process and both serve vital functions.

In the wake of recent Wall Street problems and the mortgage lending crisis, all lending decisions became tougher and business lending dried up. As such, many businesspeople also started looking at local credit unions as a funding option. This became even more after Congress passed a bill that created a multibillion-dollar fund to spur community bank lending to small businesses. All of which is to say, lending is up at these institutions. Indeed, even though community banks make up only 12 percent of all banks, they are now making in excess of 20 percent of all small business loans. (And 50 percent of all loans for under $100,000 are made by community banks too.) So the good news is that you now have two options when it comes to bank loans—regular, national banks and community banks too. Both are good and both are viable.

> **What to look for in a community bank: Are they friendly and personal? This should be near the top of your list. It is that personal attention that helps foster a close working relationship with a banker, and that may help you when lending time comes. Do they understand your business? Many community banks specialize in certain local industries. What is its reputation in the community? This is also an important factor.**

Community banks are apt to say yes to a small business loan request for a variety of reasons:

- *They are smaller.* Community banks and credit unions can be responsive since you both work and live in the same community. The bankers may even know you already or patronize your business.
- *They may be more flexible.* These banks may be more able to try new ideas, forms of collateral, and loan formats in order to help you get funded.
- *They are local.* As such, they are well positioned to lend to their bread-and-butter clients, the locally owned small business.
- *Funds are available.* In the next chapter we look at SBA loans in detail, but it is important to mention here that community banks and credit unions are big in the SBA loan business. They want to help you get that SBA-backed loan.

Bottom Line: Banks still say yes, but are able to do so less often than they used to. Nevertheless, by understanding the Four Cs of credit and utilizing options like co-signers, you can still get one of those great conventional bank loans.

CHAPTER 3

SBA Loans

Essential Idea: Obtain a Bank Loan Guaranteed by the Small Business Administration

Jesse Kresky founded the Kresky Manufacturing Company in Petaluma, California, in the early 1900s. In 1953, the Kreskys diversified their business and created Kresky Signs. The company became a leader and innovator in the industry as it pioneered the mass-production of fabricated signs for a national market. Kresky became the first supplier of baked enamel metal signs in the western United States—the big, famous red Coca-Cola button sign was one of its products.

Although the manufacturing arm of Kresky moved to Southern California in the 1970s, the sign company stayed in Northern California. When the founder passed away, his son took over, and when the son passed away in 2009, his sister Cecilia Miller took the reins of the company. Miller soon realized that Kresky Signs had not updated its equipment in quite some time. She decided that she needed to get a loan for that purpose, as well as for working capital and marketing.

Her loan options looked challenging in 2010; that is, until she started working with a lender that offered SBA loans. In short order, Miller qualified for and received an SBA loan. And because of special incentives available at the time, the six-figure loan Kresky Signs received even came with a fee waiver. Miller was thrilled with the loan as it was affordable and the terms were great. The business continues to thrive to this day (over

500 customers, 10 employees), thanks in part to that easy and affordable SBA loan.

It is the sort of success story the SBA strives for.

SBA LOANS

What if I were to tell you that there is an agency of the United States government whose sole job is to help you succeed in your business? Would you like that? And what if I further told you that said agency facilitates in excess of 50,000 small business loans a year, totaling more than $15 billion? Do you think that may help you get your business funded?

I thought so.

Of course we are talking about the Small Business Administration. In many ways, the SBA is one of the best friends your business can have, but this is even truer when it comes to funding. SBA loans have helped millions of entrepreneurs start and grow their business and they can help you too.

The first thing to understand about SBA loans is that the SBA does not make loans, as strange as that sounds. What the SBA does is *guarantee loans*. By offering a loan guarantee to a bank, the SBA makes it easier for that bank to make more loans since the bank is assured of repayment; if the borrower is unable to repay the loan, the US government will. That is a fine incentive for making more loans.

Now, why does the SBA do this? The answer is that it wants to spur business development. The federal government knows that small business really is the backbone of the US economy. Accordingly, the more loans that are made to qualified small businesses, the greater the positive economic ripple effect will be:

- More startups begin.
- More businesses grow.
- More jobs are created.

So getting funds into the hands of qualified small businesses helps business, helps the economy, and helps generate more tax revenue.

You may have noticed that I keep using the phrase "qualified small businesses." The interesting thing here is that qualifying for an SBA loan is different, and easier, than qualifying for a traditional bank loan. Because it is the job of the SBA to get more businesses in business, SBA loan standards are eased. There is more money for startups, for example.

This is not to say that it is easy to get an SBA loan. "Easier" is a more apt description. SBA.gov puts it this way: "While the standards for SBA-qualifying loans are more flexible than those for other types of loans, lenders still require extensive documentation to evaluate your loan request."

So it is important to understand a few things up front:

- First, do not expect to get 100 percent financing from the SBA. That doesn't happen. You will need to have some of your own skin in the game if you want to play ball with the SBA. According to SBA.gov, "Business loan applicants must have a reasonable amount of capital invested in their business. This ensures that, when combined with borrowed funds, the business can operate on a sound basis. Lenders will expect you to contribute your own assets and to undertake personal financial risk to establish the business before asking them to commit any funding. If you have a significant personal investment in the business, you are more likely to do everything in your power to make the business successful."
- Second, you will need to show you are profitable. "A company must be able to meet all its debt payments, not just its loan payments, as they come due. All SBA loans require that the borrower be able to reasonably demonstrate the ability to repay the intended obligation from the business operation."
- Third, the welcome news is that you may not need collateral. "To the extent that worthwhile assets are available, adequate collateral is required as security on all SBA loans. However, SBA will generally not decline a loan where inadequacy of collateral is the only unfavorable factor."
- The Four Cs matter. "Character is the personal impression you make on the potential lender or investor. The lender decides subjectively whether or not you are sufficiently trustworthy to repay the loan or generate a return on funds invested in your company. Managerial

capacity is an important factor, and your educational background and experience in business and in your industry will be reviewed. The quality of your references and the background and experience of your employees will also be considered."

Finally, in all likelihood, you will need to sign a personal guarantee if you want to secure an SBA loan.

"Bank of America, betting on companies that weathered the economic slowdown, said it increased lending about 25 percent" to small and medium business in the first half of 2010. "The bank loaned $45.4 billion through the end of June, or almost $9 billion more than in the same period a year ago," said Robb Hilson, a B of A spokesperson. At the same time, the bank is also emphasizing client satisfaction because it is good business.

Source: Bloomberg News, July 28, 2010.

TYPES OF SBA LOANS

There are many SBA loans and many programs. Here are the main ones:

7(a) Loan. This is the basic, mainstay SBA loan program. The 7(a) loans can be used for all sorts of things—startups, working capital, equipment, furniture, and even real estate. The length of the loan can be anywhere from 10 to 25 years, and loan amounts have recently been raised to $5 million.

Microloan Program. As opposed to the rest of the world where a microloan is typically for a few hundred dollars, microloans in the United States (at least SBA microloans) can be for as much as $50,000. Money here can be used for working capital or for the purchase of furniture, supplies, inventory, fixtures, or equipment. You cannot buy real estate with microloans. In the case of a microloan, the funds are typically distributed through nonprofit, community-based lenders (as opposed to larger financial institutions).

How much does the SBA guarantee? Traditionally, SBA loan guarantees worked this way:

- Loans up to $50,000: SBA guarantees 50 percent of the loan.
- Loans up to $150,000: SBA guarantees 85 percent of the loan.
- Loans above $150,000: SBA guarantees 75 percent of the loan.

A big change resulting from the 2009 stimulus law is that the SBA now has the right to guarantee up to 90 percent of all loans. Sometimes the SBA does in fact guarantee that much, but not always. As they say, "your results may vary."

Certified Development Company (CDC)/504 Loan Program. The CDC/504 loan program offers long-term, fixed-rate loans for real estate and machinery purchases, or for modernization and expansion. The typical 504 loan works this way: The business contributes at least 10 percent of the funds, a private lender funds approximately 50 percent, and the 504 loan covers 40 percent. The 504 share of the deal usually goes up as high as $1.5 million, but can go up to $2 million (i. e., a $5 million project) if the project "satisfies a public policy goal."

Express Loans (Community Express, Patriot Express, SBA Express). Express loans are just that—fast loans. Part of the 7(a) program, the difference is that Express loan decisions are made within 36 hours, and the SBA, not the lender, makes the decision. Loans are guaranteed up to 50 percent. Collateral is not required for loans under $25,000. Maximum loan amount for SBA Express loans is $350,000.

The Community Express loans generally apply to loans in areas included in Historically Underutilized Business Zones (HUBZones) and distressed communities that are part of the Community Reinvestment Act (CRA). Maximum loan amount is $250,000. Patriot Express loans are for small businesses that are 51 percent or more owned/controlled by veterans or who are part of the military community. Maximum loan amount is $500,000.

Military Reservist Loans. Military Reservist Economic Injury Disaster Loans (MREIDLs) are for small businesses that need help meeting ordinary and necessary operating expenses that they are unable to meet because an essential employee is called up to military active duty.

Export loans. The SBA has set up three different export loan programs designed to help applicable small businesses (usually 20 employees or less) expand their exports activities. The following programs vary, of course, depending on your size and needs:

1. ExportExpress
2. Export Working Capital Program
3. International Trade Loan Program

Disaster Assistance Loan Program. Disaster assistance loans provide low-interest loans for damage to real estate, personal property, inventory, machinery and equipment, and other business assets that have been damaged or destroyed in a declared disaster.

Because of how poorly the government responded to Hurricane Katrina, the Disaster Assistance Loan Program was overhauled. According to WhiteHouse.gov, the changes are these:

• The average processing time for disaster loans went from over 70 days to just 10 days.
• Disaster victims can now apply for help online. Thirty percent choose this method.
• The number of disaster loan processing centers jumped from 366 to 1,750 workstations.
• The number of SBA disaster staff from went from 800 to 1,200.

The SBA has one other program that you should know. The "Loan Prequalification" program will analyze your loan package (up to $250,000) before you take it to a lender. An SBA-designated liaison will review your application, offer suggestions, help make corrections, and generally strengthen your submission.

APPLYING FOR AN SBA LOAN

There really is not a lot of difference between applying for an SBA loan and applying for a conventional business loan. You will need to provide extensive documentation as to your need and use of the monies and you will need to make a great impression. The main difference is that here, you will need to fill out SBA forms in addition to whatever else the lender typically requires.

The basic SBA forms that you should expect to encounter, among others, are the following:

- Form 4: Application for Business Loan
- Form 4A: Schedule of Collateral
- Form 413: Personal Financial Statement
- Form 912: Statement of Personal History
- Form 1846: Statement Regarding Lobbying

Again, although lender loan requirements vary, you should expect that your SBA loan package should include the following. (Note that some of these items are covered in the loan proposal package that was discussed in the last chapter. It is equally applicable here too.)

Executive Summary. As with your business plan, your SBA loan proposal should begin with an executive summary that highlights who you are, what your business is, the amount and purpose of the loan, and how you expect to repay it and when. Put your best foot forward!

Business Profile. Describe your business, its background, sales figures, number of employees, the competition, your vendors, and your competitive advantage.

Management Team. Do not underestimate how important this is. Lenders and investors will often look to the strength of your management team first when analyzing a business.

Repayment Terms. Cash flow statements and budgets should be included here to explain how the loan will be repaid, from what sources, and by when.

Collateral, Form 4A. Many small business loans are secured using the home(s) of the principal(s).

Personal Financial Statement, Form 413. The SBA requires financial statements from all owners, officers, partners, and shareholders. Include tax returns for the previous three years.

Business Financial Statements. Include profit and loss statements, balance sheets, income statements, schedule of debts, and accounts receivable. Startups are reminded that grossly inflated financials will work against them.

Projections. Include business projections for at least one year out. Explain assumptions.

Other. Include appropriate leases, contracts, purchase orders, Articles of Incorporation, partnership agreements, and letters of reference.

If you have any questions, contact your local SBA district office. They will be happy to help.

Bottom Line: SBA loans are one of your best options when looking for funding for your business.

CHAPTER 4

Equity Line of Credit

Essential Idea: Use Equity in Your Home or Business to Obtain a Line of Credit from a Bank

Brian was not the greatest businessperson in the world. Sure, he had a nice wedding photography business that netted him a decent income every month, but Brian was not much for budgets. And given that Brian's was a seasonal enterprise, his inability to put money away for the fallow seasons of his business was a yearly problem.

His ingenious solution (or so he thought) was to use credit cards to live on during the winter months, when work was scarce. And how did he pay off the credit cards? Home equity. Brian lived in Los Angeles and had bought his little house back when it was still relatively affordable. All through the 1990s and into the 2000s, Brian's home went up, up, up in value.

He thought it would never stop.

So every few years, after having run up his credit cards and other debts, Brian would refinance his house using his increased home equity, pay off his debt, and go along his merry way. And then, around 2006 or so, Brian realized he could save money and make things even easier by simply getting an equity line of credit, which he did, for both business and personal use.

Well, you can imagine what happened. By 2008, Brian owed about $80,000 on his line of credit. But that was the year the housing market fell off a cliff and banks froze or canceled many lines of credit. Brian ended up filing for bankruptcy.

Are equity lines of credit still available? Sure. Do you need to use extreme caution when you use this tool? Right again.

EQUITY LINES OF CREDIT

There are all sorts of ways to structure a deal for capital for your business. More often than not, the money comes in as a lump sum, as in the case of a business loan. But lump sum payments are not the only game in town. Not infrequently, businesses need capital on an ongoing, consistent basis.

Example: A business may have a several-month lag between the time it buys inventory and sells those products. In that case, and in the meantime, the business may need money for operations, payroll, you name it, and yet with goods unsold, cash flow becomes an issue. In that case the answer often is to obtain a line of credit.

In some rare cases, when the owners and business have a great track record and outstanding credit, that line of credit may be unsecured. But as you can imagine, that is fairly rare. Unsecured lines of credit are risky, and as has been discussed previously, banks dislike risk.

As such, the more common practice is to secure the line of credit with some sort of equity. Generally speaking, there are two types of equity lines of credit: a business equity line of credit and a home equity line of credit. But in reality, these are distinctions without a difference. In practice, the two types of equity lines work in essentially the same way. The difference, of course, is what sort of collateral is used to secure the credit line—a business asset or the home of one of the owners. Almost always, using business assets as collateral beats using your house.

It helps to think of an equity credit line as a sort of secured credit card. The credit is there, available to use when you need it, if you need it. During the life of the loan, you can use as much or as little of the credit line as you need. And, as the principle is paid down, more credit becomes available, as with a credit card.

> An equity line of credit is not the same thing as an equity loan. An equity loan will result in you receiving a lump sum payment with a specific due date. An equity line of credit will not put cash in your pocket upon closing, only credit, and the due date is more flexible.

There are definitely pros and cons to this funding option.

Pros
- As opposed to some other types of loans, an equity credit line can be used for almost any business purpose.
- The terms will be better than you would find on a credit card.
- Equity lines are a form of revolving credit. There are often two periods associated with an equity line of credit—the "draw period" and the "repayment period." During the draw period, when you can draw funds from the credit line, you can use the loan as much or as little as you need. As long as you make your payments and service the loan, the credit line stays in effect. During the repayment period, you cannot access the credit line.

But all that said, the downsides are not insignificant.

Cons
- A home equity loan is a second mortgage. As such, the biggest downside, and the main reason why a home equity line of credit is a very risky option, is that the collateral is your house (as opposed to a business equity line of credit, where the collateral is some business asset). If your business goes south and you are unable to repay the equity loan, the bank will repossess your home. That is a huge risk, and often too much of a risk.
- In addition, equity lines of credit fluctuate. First, they fluctuate because interest rates will change over the course of the loan. These are not fixed loans. Second, because the equity in an asset can fluctuate, so too can the line of credit. As you know, equity is the difference between how much an asset is worth and how much you owe on it. If you bought a house for $200,000 and you owe $125,000, there is $75,000 in equity. But if the real estate market crashes and all of a sudden the house is worth only $135,000, then you have only $10,000 in equity. If you have a line of credit tied to that depreciating house, that can be big trouble for your business.

HOW IT WORKS

A typical equity line of credit can be for anywhere between, say, $25,000 and $1 million; could be more, could be less. The collateralized real estate in all likelihood will need to be either owner occupied or investment property, although in a commercial setting, the collateral could also be accounts receivable or tangible business assets such as equipment or vehicles. The approval process should be fairly quick, less than a month, certainly. Once approved, you will receive a checkbook and a credit card tied to the credit line so that you can access the capital in a way that works best for you.

How much credit will you get? Let's say that you need an equity line of credit and decide for some reason to use your home as collateral. How much credit should you expect to be extended to you? Many lenders, especially today, limit lines of credit to, say, no more than 75 percent of the home's appraised value, and then subtract from that the mortgage to calculate the credit line. For the sake of argument, let's say that:

The house is valued at	$100,000
times 0.75 equals	$ 75,000
And you still owe	$ 50,000
So you might get an equity line of	$ 25,000

If you (wisely) use a business asset as collateral, the analysis is still roughly similar.

Costs. There are several fees that you will pay when applying for and receiving an equity line of credit. Aside from the typical bank fees (application fee, document preparation fees, etc.) expect to also pay for a property appraisal, a title search, and so forth.

After funding, the amount you pay each month will depend upon how much of the credit you use and the state of your variable interest rate. The variable rate depends upon (1) your credit and (2) the prime rate (i.e., the rate charged to banks to borrow money from the Fed). The lender will add its margin to the prime rate and that will be your interest rate.

Adjustments to the variable interest rate you will pay on your equity line of credit can be made monthly, quarterly, or yearly. Be sure to negotiate, and understand, this detail before signing any paperwork. There will also be a cap on how high the interest rate can go. Know and negotiate (if possible) this important fact too.

Finally, expect to pay monthly fees as well: maintenance charges, per transaction fees, and yes, even inactivity fees if you do not use the credit line.

Repayment. The amount of time you will have to repay your line of credit depends upon the loan terms, of course. Some credit lines require that you make interest-only payments during the draw period while others ask that you make combined principal and interest payments. The problem with an interest-only repayment schedule is that you will still owe a lump sum principal payment upon completion of the loan. Because of that, it is almost always the smarter course of action to make principal and interest payments on your loan. The more principal you pay off sooner, the less interest you will have to pay over the life of the loan.

One note of caution with regard to home equity lines of credit: If you sell your home you will likely have to pay off your equity line immediately, or as part of the closing of the sale. Given that, be sure that the home equity line of credit choice makes sense for both your business and your life plans.

Bottom Line: Equity lines of credit are risky options, and especially risky if secured by your personal residence. Try to avoid this option unless you have a way to get the credit line that is not tied to your home.

CHAPTER 5

Credit Cards

Essential Idea: Use Credit Cards to Fund Your Business

Credit cards can be one of the best ways to fund a business because they are both easy to use and so flexible. When used intelligently, credit cards can really be a boon to your business. You just need to be smart about it.

Back when I was a practicing lawyer, my specialties were business and bankruptcy law. The vast majority of my bankruptcy clients had one common denominator: they got in over their heads with credit card debt. These folks certainly never planned on this, of course; in fact, most loved and appreciated their credit cards. Indeed, many had credit card indebtedness that was not unreasonable at all, but something happened in their life to tip the balance:

- Maybe they lost their job.
- Or possibly they got divorced.
- They may have had a medical emergency.
- Maybe they were sued.

Whatever the case, all of a sudden that manageable credit card debt became unmanageable and there they were, sitting in my office.

The one exception was Joe (name changed). I remember him vividly because, while he too had his share of credit card debt, he was just so different than the rest. Debt was not his problem and not why he hired me, although at any given time, he had plenty of debt.

No, Joe hired me for my business expertise. Joe wanted to expand and needed help negotiating a lease on the new facility. But when he told me that he was planning on financing his business expansion with credit cards, I nearly blew a gizzard. Given my background with all of my other clients, I strongly advised Joe against that plan. But Joe had a great motto:

"Not all debt is bad debt," he used to say.

Joe was a crafty businessman who knew exactly what he was doing. He had a stellar credit rating and sterling cards with squat rates to prove it. He financed his business with credit cards because they were easy to get and easy to use, and he did not have to impress any "fancy-pants bankers" (his words) to run his business his way. And because he had a great credit rating, the cards were affordable. Joe had a very specific plan, never ran the cards up too high, and always paid them off every few months. Here was a guy who knew how to use credit cards the right way, the smart way.

CREDIT CARDS AND YOUR BUSINESS

Pop quiz! What do you think are the two most common funding methods entrepreneurs use when starting their ventures? If you said "friends and family" and "credit cards," then congratulations! You get to pass Go and collect $200 (or maybe $20,000). According to a recent survey by the Pioneer Institute, those two funding sources are the most popular startup financing strategies. And it is not hard to see why. Friends and family members usually offer very easy terms, and credit cards are readily available.

In fact, there are a lot of great things to be said about using a credit card to fund your business. You do not need to show your business plan to a bank and get them to sign off on it and you do not need to convince an investor that yours is the best idea since sliced bread. You don't have to barter away equity in your company and you don't have to be turned down by people who don't get you. You can use the cards when and where you like and to the extent you can afford. So it is not surprising that credit cards are a popular choice.

The important thing, however, is to use them wisely. Whether you use your own credit or that of your business usually depends upon your situation and needs. Startups typically have no business credit so the entrepreneur is forced to use his or her own credit to fund the business. More mature companies will likely have a credit history and, as such, using a business credit card is more doable. In any case, it's a better way to go.

Let's examine both scenarios.

USING YOUR OWN CREDIT CARDS FOR BUSINESS

There are both upsides and downsides to using personal credit cards to fund your business venture. On the plus side, credit cards are easy to use and flexible:

- They provide quick access to ready capital.
- Depending upon your situation, you may have access to a lot of credit.
- You can transfer balances in order to get low interest rates.
- Repayment occurs monthly, over a long period of time.
- You don't have to wait to get funding; in fact, you need no one's approval at all to get started.

Those are all significant benefits and fine reasons. It is easy to see why entrepreneurs so often turn to credit cards to fund their dream.

Having said that, the list of potential problems when using credit cards for your business is equally impressive:

- It is sometimes easy to get in over your head with credit cards.
- Interest rates can jump.
- Credit lines can be terminated.
- Because you need not prove your plan to anyone before using your available credit, the cards have the chance of being run up on ideas that have no business getting funded.

There are two more major problems that come with using personal credit cards to fund business endeavors. The first is the many dangers that come from commingling personal and business finances. First of all, if things go south, commingling endangers your personal assets and personal credit. In addition, if you are ever audited, commingling is not something the IRS likes to see. Similarly, if you are ever sued, commingling is evidence that your corporation is but a shell and should possibly be voided. This is called "piercing the corporate veil." We do not like it when our corporate veil is pierced. And finally, keeping your business finances separate from your personal finances allows you to build your business credit profile.

But the most significant downside when using your own credit cards to fund your business, and the biggest risk, is that you will be personally liable for business debts. Given that one of the main, and very basic, reasons to incorporate is to protect your personal assets from business liabilities, putting your own credit and assets at risk by using your personal credit cards to fund your business is not highly recommended.

Of course, as an entrepreneur, you are an optimist—that seems to be part of the job description. And while that is often great, and enthusiasm can open a lot of doors, having a blue-sky mentality can also be risky when it comes to startups and finances. Why?

Startups do not always succeed.

But although businesses do fail and close their doors, unfortunately, that personal credit card debt does not end with the venture. So we have to be smart about how we use credit cards. Here's how:

- *Use cards with the lowest interest rate first.* Charging the most money on the card with the lowest interest rate is smart; you will pay less in interest. If you have several cards with low rates, use them evenly. If only one card has a low rate, use it first, and make sure that the rate is not set to rise anytime soon (i.e., after an introductory teaser rate expires).

  As you proceed, consider applying for some new cards that do in fact have some introductory teaser rates. These will be valuable for a balance transfer. Also, down the road, you may be able to negotiate with the credit card company to keep these cards at the lower rate, but in any case, the longer you can be charged less using cards with low rates, the better.

It also helps to plan ahead and clean up your credit before extensively using your credit cards. It is estimated that well over half of all credit reports contain errors, and errors mean higher interest rates for you. Credit reporting agencies are required to remove an error within 30 days once you prove it in writing.

The Fair Credit Reporting Act (FCRA) requires each of the nationwide consumer credit reporting companies—Equifax, Experian, and TransUnion—to provide you with a free copy of your credit report, at your request, once every 12 months. To order yours, visit annualcreditreport.com or call 1-877-322-8228.

- *Be prudent.* Starting a new business is exciting and it is easy to get caught up in the moment, especially when you have available credit to use. It is not hard to end up charging for things that are more want than need.

    Slow down there, cowboy. Take your time. Be prudent.

    My brother sells real estate for a living. He has a phrase for that moment when a buyer so falls in love with a property that he or she stops thinking rationally and starts to think emotionally. It is called "falling under the ether." We have all fallen under the ether, whether it is for a home, a new car, or that new smartphone. This feeling can be fun, but you rarely make smart business decisions in that state. So the important thing is to avoid falling under the ether and to use your credit cards wisely, prudently, and with a plan, like my old client Joe.

    When the bill comes at the end of the month, you will be happy you did.

- *Be careful.* These days, credit card companies sometimes cancel cards and reduce limits without a lot of warning. They especially do so when the cards are used a lot more than usual. Therefore, by running up your personal credit cards to start or grow your business, you may be sending the exact wrong signal to your card issuers and they may close out your cards before you even get started. Again, prudent is the way to go.

The important thing is that you need to be smart, cautious, and savvy when choosing to run up your credit cards in pursuit of your dream. When you have credit cards at your disposal, the good news is that the credit is easily available. The bad news is that credit is easily available. Be smart.

USING BUSINESS CREDIT CARDS

All things considered, if you have a choice between using your personal credit cards and using your business credit cards to fund your business, using the business cards always makes more sense. First of all, it avoids all of the common pitfalls previously mentioned that come from commingling. Additionally, using a business credit card for business makes bookkeeping much simpler. It is also more professional. In addition, business credit card statements can be accounted for easily, itemized, and filed appropriately. Year-end statements from the card issuer can make taxes much simpler.

Using business credit cards offers two final benefits: First, you are often able to accumulate reward points and discounts that are available only to business customers. Finally, having a business card allows you to give cards to those employees who need them and track those expenses easily. All in all, using your business credit cards to fund your business makes a lot of sense.

That is all well and good, you say, but what if you do not have any business credit? That is a short-term problem that is fairly easily rectified. Here are the basic steps:

1. The first thing to do is to incorporate so that the business is a legal entity separate and apart from yourself.
2. Next, get a federal tax ID number from the IRS, also called an EIN (for Employer Identification Number).
3. Then open up a checking account using the business name and tax ID number. Open up a small savings account as well.
4. Use the business name and EIN number to establish basic services—telephone, Internet, FedEx accounts, that sort of thing.
5. Then, look to get a small loan from your bank—in the name of the business—secured by that business savings account. The collateral of the bank account makes approval much more likely.
6. Make sure the bank reports the loan repayment history to the credit reporting agencies, as well as Dun & Bradstreet.
7. After a year or so of this, start to apply for credit cards in the name of the business. Be sure to apply for cards that do not tie your business credit in with your personal credit, or where you personally guarantee the business credit.

If you follow this simple strategy, in a year or so, you will have a solid business credit profile and will not need to ever commingle your business and personal finances again. You can then go and get credit from Visa, MasterCard, and hopefully also American Express.

AVOIDING COMMON CREDIT CARD PROBLEMS

Whether you use your own personal cards or business cards, it still remains true that understanding how credit cards work and how to avoid some common pitfalls makes sense.

Credit card basics. When using credit cards in your business, the things to be most concerned with are:

- How much you charge.
- What the interest rate is on your outstanding balance.
- How you can pay off the balance as soon as possible.

Of course, as indicated, teaser rates are best. A teaser rate is an introductory interest rate offered by a credit card issuer to get your business. The first question to consider when looking to use a card with a teaser rate is how long the rate will last. Sometimes teaser rates can last up to a year; other times they may be for only three months.

> One businesswoman was once offered a card with a great teaser rate and a $5,000 limit. She accepted, got the card, and attempted to transfer $5,000 from a different card with a higher rate onto this new, lower card. But the transfer check bounced. Why? The new card charged a $10 transfer fee, so she went over her limit by $10. The card issuer then assessed her a $25 "bounced check" fee to boot! She had a balance of $35 and had never used the card.

One way to keep your payments low is to get the teaser rate extended for as long as possible. Here's how: before the rate is set to expire, call up the card-issuing company and ask them to extend the rate for another six months. Many will. If they refuse, there are plenty of other cards out there that offer introductory rates.

Avoiding the credit card trap. Beware of these final issues when using credit cards to fund your business:

- *High interest rates.* The average credit card interest rate is 17 percent. It is easy to charge a little but owe a lot at that rate.

- *Cash advances.* To get a cash advance on a credit card, you usually pay a transaction fee of around 3 percent per advance, and there is no grace period.
- *Fees.* Late fees, over-limit fees, underuse fees—it can all get a bit overwhelming.

Of these three, it is the first (the interest rate) that makes the biggest difference. For example, say that you owe $10,000 on your credit cards, which have an average interest rate of 16.9 percent. (Of course, your rate may be lower. If so, bully for you.) Your annual cost, between interest payments and fees, to borrow $10,000 a year would be about $2,400. But look what happens if your interest rate was "only" 8.9 percent: Your annual cost would be about $1,400; you would be saving roughly $1,000. If you had a card with something like a 5.9 percent rate, your annual savings would be about $1,300. Multiply this by each of your cards and you will begin to see some real savings.

So the first part of the credit card trap is paying too much in interest. The other big one is just paying the minimum amount due every month. Many people get their bill, look at the minimum payment due, and pay that amount. This is the absolutely biggest mistake you can make with credit cards. Minimum payments guarantee that you will pay for what you bought many times over.

Credit card billing errors do occur, but can easily be resolved if you know the law. The Fair Credit Billing Act (FCBA) allows consumers to challenge disputes over credit card bills. Pursuant to the FCBA, if you ever see a mistake on your credit card statement, write the company a letter explaining the problem. They then have 30 days to begin to investigate the matter and respond. If an error is found, the FCBA mandates that the creditor write to you, explain the corrections it will make to your account, and remedy the error. Similarly, if they conclude there was no mistake, you must be told this in writing too and be given an explanation.

Example: Say that you have a credit card with a $9,000 balance, and an interest rate of 17 percent. How long will it take you to pay it off, given the minimum payment of 2 percent? Let's do a little math. A monthly minimum payment of 2 percent on a 17 percent card with a $9,000 balance is $165. So, if you paid just the minimum, your balance the next month would start at $8,835. If you continued to pay the minimum, it would take you (get ready for this) over 40 years to pay off the entire card. And you would also end up paying almost $18,000 on your $9,000 balance. So paying the minimum payment on your credit cards is the biggest mistake you can make.

Look at what happens when you pay more than just the minimum. In the $9,000 example, the 2 percent minimum payment amount goes down every month as the principal decreases. However, if you keep paying the original minimum payment of $165 instead of the new, lower minimum, you will decrease the time it takes to reduce your credit card debt from 40 years to just about five years. If you could increase the payment from $165 to $265, that $9,000 debt would be repaid in just less than three years.

Thus, the key to using credit cards wisely when charging for business needs is to pay more than the minimum every month; pay as much as you can afford.

Bottom Line: When used smartly, credit cards are an incredible funding option. But lack of attention to the details of the card or debt can be very dangerous to your enterprise.

CHAPTER **6**

The Friends and Family Plan

Essential Idea: Get the Money You Need from Your Extended Clan

It is January of 1980, and the unemployment rate is a whopping 7.5 percent (and soon to soar above 10 percent). Inflation is an even more astounding 13 percent. Undoubtedly it is the worst economy in 50 years. Against this bleak backdrop, two out-of-work journalists have an epiphany one night that changes their world, and that of their closest friends and family members too.

Chris Haney and Scott Abbott loved to play Scrabble, and with plenty of time on their hands (being out of work and all), Scrabble they played. One night they pulled the game out of the closet and discovered that one of the tiny alphabet tiles of their set was missing. So Haney and Abbott hopped in the car and headed off to the toy store to buy another Scrabble set.

And then it hit them—they had bought a lot of Scrabble games over the years, and there had to be a lot of other people who were doing the same thing every day. Even better, they surmised, in a bad economy people were looking to save money by entertaining at home. What they needed to do, Haney and Abbott decided, was to invent a new board game. And they even thought they had a great idea for one.

That there had not been a new board game invented in many, many years did not deter them. (Scrabble and Monopoly were about it at the time.) But the two friends faced other problems—both initially and over the long haul. The main one was that they were broke and unemployed. How could they start a business, create their game, and then market that game with no money?

They needed investors.

But getting a bank loan, being in the position they were in, was next to impossible. Similarly, finding an angel investor was out of the question given their circumstances. No, they knew their only hope was to approach friends and family with their great idea and a solid plan for executing on that idea. So that is what they did.

They drafted a simple business plan and began to approach their extended network. They explained what the game was and what their plan was for marketing it. Eventually, they scraped together about $60,000 from 32 friends, family members, associates, and colleagues, each of whom received a 1 percent share of the nascent company for their faith and investment.

The outcome?

Less than two years later the game Haney and Abbott would invent became a national obsession, with no less than Johnny Carson raving about it on *The Tonight Show*. The game? A little something called Trivial Pursuit. (Side note: Can you imagine owning 1 percent of Trivial Pursuit for a mere $2,000 investment?!)

THE UBIQUITOUS OPTION

It is probably safe to say that many, if not most, small businesses begin with at least some funding from friends and/or family members. It could be a gift of money from dad or a low-interest loan from Lew, but whatever the case, a capital infusion from someone close can often mean the difference between launching and flailing.

A report from Angel Capital Education Foundation says that the total amount of investment stemming from venture capitalists, state funds, and angel investors is roughly $20 billion a year. The amount from friends and family? About three times that amount.

It is not hard to understand why people turn to family and friends. Ready money and sweet deals are hard to beat, especially when startups have no track record. They have no sales. They have little equity, and often no collateral. What they do have is an enthusiastic entrepreneur with a super idea, a lot of promises, and even more hope. But since hope doesn't pay the bills, and charisma cannot collateralize a loan, mom and dad are often the funding choice of first, and last, resort.

It doesn't hurt either that a yes may not be that hard to get, or that they believe in your vision and are willing to give you some pretty incredible terms. Indeed, many a family loan includes terms that are otherwise unheard of: repayment beginning only after the business starts to turn a profit, interest rates at 0 percent, forgiveness of outstanding debts after a certain amount of time, and so forth. Yes, it is all great.

Or is it?

The answer is no, it is not all great, not by a long shot. Sure, money from people who love you can be a welcome oasis in the dry desert that can be business funding, but if not handled properly, the money can be more mirage than watering hole.

Take it from someone who learned somewhat the hard way: If you treat a business investment from someone close to you with all of the seriousness it deserves, and if you repay it in a timely fashion, it is indeed a gift from the gods. But if you are too casual about the arrangement (and many entrepreneurs who receive family funding are), you can cause stress to yourself, and worse, to the people who believed in you.

If something is too good to be true, it is. But if you are smart, prudent, and professional, all can go well.

THE GOOD NEWS

As you begin to think about finding funding from a loved one, consider the relative positions you are both in.

What's in it for you? Of course the obvious answer is money. Being able to get the money you need from a loved one is a blessing. You are blessed that someone loves you so much that they are willing to take a risk on you, and that they believe in what you are doing.

Yes, those are good things, but interestingly, I would also venture that if most small businesspeople had their druthers, they would prefer not to take out a loan from the bank of mom and dad. Yes, great terms are wonderful, but anyone sophisticated enough to start or run a business knows that money *always* comes with strings attached, either implied or expressed. When people invest in you, you owe them not only money, but answers. Why are you doing that? Why don't you do this? Why aren't you selling more? Seemingly innocent questions may not seem so innocent anymore.

So what's in it for you is a double-edged sword. You may get the money you so desperately need, but it will come at some price to your autonomy and relationship.

> One way to structure the deal is as a limited partnership. In that sort of arrangement, the limited partner is essentially a passive investor and has no legal say in the day-to-day operations of the business.

What's in it for them? They love you, that's what! They want to help you, help you dream, and help you get ahead. That they may make a little money on the deal is nice too. Do they think your relationship is going to change? No, probably not. And it should not, not if you handle this deal properly. Since what they want is to be a mensch, it is your job to not take advantage of their kindness, to not borrow more than you need, and to treat their investment like the business deal it is. Do that and all should be well.

THE BAD NEWS

Borrowing money from someone you know well is fraught with danger and many a relationship has ended because of it. Of course you think you have a great plan, and you well may, but there is a reason that banks are reluctant to loan money to new startups; namely, they are risky and the chance of being repaid in full and on time is not as high as the bank would like. It is that very risk that is the danger here. If you are able to repay the debt as agreed upon, then all will be fine. But it is when someone cannot or does not that problems arise.

The important thing is to be prudent. Don't ask for the money unless you have a solid plan for paying it back. Don't ask for the money unless you really *do* plan on paying it back. Don't ask for the money if the person you are asking cannot really afford it. Don't ask for more money than they can afford, or can safely afford to lose. Don't ask for more money than you need. Don't borrow the money with an "I will get it back to you someday" attitude.

This should be viewed as more business deal and less personal favor, rather than the other way around.

The other thing of which to be aware, even if and as you do repay the loan on time, is that borrowing money from a loved one will change your relationship to one degree or another. The mixing of one's personal life with one's business life, whatever the circumstances, affects both. It is not unlike dating someone from the office—it changes things. Money changes things.

Have I scared you yet? Good, let's hope so.

HOW TO APPROACH A FAMILY MEMBER

Before approaching any friend or family member, the first thing to do is to draft a plan. It need not be a formal business plan (although that is all the better), but it does need to be some sort of plan that explains what the business is, what the investment is, what your proposed terms of the deal are, and when it will be repaid. Not only will this give them comfort and more reason to say yes, but it will also give you the confidence to ask.

Once you have your (full or mini) business plan ready, the next step is to call the person in question. Let them know what you are considering and set up a meeting. Treat it as you would a meeting with any other investor: Be on time, professional, and prepared. Explain what the venture is, why it will be successful, and how you see it proceeding.

Consider the questions your friend may ask:

- How risky is this venture?
- Who else is investing in it?
- How much of your own money do you have invested?
- When should they expect to see their money back?

One word of caution: avoid making unrealistic promises. You will surely want to impress them, but you will have a better chance of doing that with honest assessments that in turn yield realistic expectations. Overinflating your offer can only lead to an overinflated outlook. Remember the old adage: *underpromise and overdeliver.*

The more you treat your loved one like a businessperson and less like a loved one, the more they will treat you that way too.

STRUCTURING THE DEAL

If and when you get to the place where Grandma wants to lend you some money, here is how to put the deal together in a way that protects you both:

Decide what sort of deal it is. As you know by now, a deal like this can be either a debt deal, whereby you are taking on debt for a loan, or an equity deal, whereby you are selling part of your company for the investment. You need to know which it is.

Loan or gift? The other possibility is that the money is a gift. That, of course, solves many of the issues raised earlier, and in addition, may even provide the giver with some tax benefits. Currently, someone can give a gift of up to $13,000 a year without it being a taxable event. Check with your lawyer.

Clearly define the arrangement. While I have said plenty about the risks to the lender, it is also important to consider the risks to you, the entrepreneur. The major one is that your family member may expect to have some sort of say in the running of your business in exchange for the money. Most entrepreneurs don't want that.

If you really want to impress that family member, consider formalizing your arrangement using a third party. For example, LendingKarma.com is an online site that "lays the proper groundwork to help your loan succeed and remove some of the pressure that goes with the personal lending process. We help you to:

- Calculate a payment schedule that works for both the borrower(s) and the lender(s)
- Clearly define and document all loan terms
- Track the loan all the way through repayment with payment tracking and friendly email payment reminders"

Put it in writing. Put everything in writing—all essential terms, dates, amounts, and so forth. I know you know this, but make sure you do it. Memories fade over time, people remember things differently, and yes, some people lie. A written document prevents all of that from happening. Things to add to this list are:

- Names of the parties
- Amount of the investment
- Interest rates and due dates
- Collateral, if any
- What will happen in the case of default, or the death or incapacity of either party
- The roles of each party

Bottom Line: Getting the money from friends or family can be a great financial deal, but keep in mind the potential emotional ramifications.

CHAPTER 7

Angel Investors

Essential Idea: Get Funding from High Net Worth Individuals

In 1982, Andy Bechtolsheim cofounded the computer company Sun Microsystems. Sun was an almost instant success, earning more than $1 billion in sales by 1988. In 1995, Bechtolsheim left Sun and founded Granite Systems. A year later, Cisco Systems acquired Granite for $220 million. An already rich man, Bechtolsheim was suddenly much richer.

In 1996, Larry Page and Sergey Brin were PhD students at Stanford and had started working on a research project that analyzed the mathematical underpinnings of the Internet. Specifically, they wanted to look at how to categorize the usefulness of websites using, among other things, the number and quality of sites that linked to a particular page. Using mathematical algorithms, Page and Brin soon saw that the pages that had the most sites linking to them on a given subject were among the most relevant in a search engine query; after all, if a lot of sites linked to a page, that page must be useful, right? This was a revolutionary insight at the time. Page and Brin then decided to use this information to create their own search engine, using, at first, the Stanford website. The URL? Google.stanford.edu.

The URL Google.com was not registered until the next year, 1997, and the company did not even incorporate until 1998. Even then, it did so only because it had to. The reason was that Page and Brin met Andy Bechtolsheim in 1998, gave him a demonstration of Google, and he decided to invest in their nascent company. Bechtolsheim wrote out a check in the amount of $100,000 to "Google, Inc." Given that Brin and Page had been financing the startup with credit cards up until that point, this was an extraordinary turn of events. According to *Contacto Magazine* (September 28, 2006, *"Once upon a Time . . . Google Was Born"*), "The investment created a small dilemma. There was no way to deposit the check since there was no legal entity known as 'Google, Inc.' It sat in Larry's desk drawer for a couple of weeks while he and Sergey scrambled to set up a corporation."

The rest, as they say, is history. That $100,000 angel investment by Bechtolsheim soon led to almost another million in investor funding. In 1999, the venture capital firms Kleiner Perkins Caufield & Byers and Sequoia Capital helped to raise $25 million for Google. In 2004, Google went public and raised more than $1 billion. Today, Google has been calculated as the world's most valuable brand, with a value of around $100 billion.

Of course, this is a unique story in that there is only one Google, but it is also a very ordinary story in another sense: A savvy investor saw an opportunity, bet on it, and it paid off handsomely. That's angel investing.

Is your business ready for an angel investment? It depends on where you are in the business and funding cycle. The usual funding process goes something like this:

- Business inspiration! Passion for the idea. Willingness to take a risk. Quitting or getting fired from the old job. Tapping into the savings account.
- Going for it. Drafting a business plan. Living on credit cards.
- Launching the business. Realizing (again, damn it!) that you no longer have any home equity. Getting a loan or cash gift from mom and dad.
- Liking this entrepreneurial thing, mostly. Getting turned down by a bank. Getting an SBA loan.
- Working too hard. Growing pains. Finding some creative funding.
- Loving what you do. Working too hard. Realizing that you still need help to take things to the next level. Reading this chapter. Getting an angel investment in your business. Recommending this great book to your friends.

After that, if smooth sailing and growth continue, and you want it, you would look at venture capital, and if you were on the path to grab the business brass ring, eventually you would look at going public.

But we are getting ahead of ourselves. Are you ready for an angel investment? Let's find out.

WHAT DO ANGELS LOOK FOR?

An angel, as the name suggests, is a high net worth individual who is willing to take a risk and invest in early-stage businesses. In exchange for an angel's monetary investment, you must be willing to give up ownership shares, power, some decision-making ability, and seats on your board; those are the price of admission if you want to play ball in the big leagues.

Angels often invest in the field from which they came, so you can find angel investors in agriculture, entertainment, restaurants, and everything in between. And as varied as the industries are, so too are the angels. Some are rich individuals looking for a smart investment, while others, increasingly, are a group of angels who have teamed up to share resources, leads, investments, and, of course, profits.

As should be apparent already, the first thing angel investors look for is the chance to make a significant return on their investment. They calculate this by looking at your business model through the prism of the following factors:

The opportunity. Why is the idea that you are presenting a great opportunity for this angel investor? Is there something special going on right now? Have you created the Next Big Thing? Do you have some sort of unfair advantage that you can exploit? Why is this a unique opportunity and how will your business capitalize on it?

An angel investment group may receive up to 100 proposals a month, some more, most much less. A good 90 percent will never even make it past the initial screening process. Of the remaining 10 percent that do, most will go through several rounds of presentations. Only one or two a month may ever see funding.

You will need to explain to the angel your *unique value proposition*. Not every business needs to be the Next Big Thing and not every business will need to raise $1 million in angel funding, but every business will need to show the investor that it offers something unique to the marketplace such that the likelihood of the investor making money is high. That is the task at hand.

The competition. Who are your competitors, and why are you better?

The financials. As indicated previously, offering wild financial projections is never a good idea. Your angel investor will want to see how you plan on spending the money, where, and on what. What are your projected sales? Why?

The team. Almost more than anything else, an investor can be wooed by a great team, one with experience, credentials, smarts, and contacts.

You. Treat your potential investors like the smart businesspeople they are. Show them that you belong. Explain how your idea, background, contacts, and experience benefit everyone.

WHERE TO FIND ANGEL INVESTORS

So the question you now probably have is, where do you locate these angel investors of which I speak? There are many ways.

The first place, and often the best, is through networking. Speak with friends and family, with your accountant and lawyer, with real estate agents, bankers, customers, and clients, with people where you worship, and with sales reps and business associates. This sort of informal networking often works well because (1) the people you speak with know you and (2) you can get a personal introduction to any potential investor.

(Note that friends and family members can also be a type of angel investor, but because they create unique opportunities and challenges, they were discussed in the previous chapter. In addition, often friends and family members offer less money than an angel might, so in that sense they are different too.)

Beyond networking, there are a variety of other options available to you:

Small Business Development Centers (SBDCs) and universities. SBDCs work in conjunction with the SBA and local universities to offer information and assistance to businesses and startups. And because the businesses that work with SBDCs are affiliated with universities (because of the SBDC connection) and because angels like that, SBDCs are a good place to look for angel investors.

And while you are at it, professors and chairs of university graduate programs in business and entrepreneurship can also be a good source for locating angel investors. They can often steer you in the right direction.

Business incubators. A business incubator is, as the name suggests, an entity that nurtures new small businesses. As with SBDCs, they are often affiliated with colleges, but not necessarily so. The typical business incubator is a public-private partnership in which entrepreneurs can get free or low-cost advice, rent, and assistance. Often associated by areas of local interest (high-tech incubators are found in Silicon Valley, for instance), business incubators can be a great place to meet angel investors who may be part of a particular incubator.

For more information about business incubators, check out the National Business Incubation Association, www.NBIA.org, and Chapter 22, "Business Incubators."

Social media. Social media is increasingly playing a significant role in matching angels and entrepreneurs, so have at it. Create a robust profile on LinkedIn and begin to network. Tweet up a storm. Create a Facebook fan page. And if you can't directly get in contact with the investor of your choice, see who they are connected to and look to connect with them. But as you do all of this, remember that the point of social networking is *not* to get as many followers as you can, but to network as well as you can. Use social media to meet people you would not otherwise normally be able to meet.

Or what about this: Blog and tweet, not about the angel, but about how great his or her projects are. That is sure to capture someone's attention.

Step by step by step you can get the money.

Angel networks. Increasingly, angels are banding together. Many of these angel investment groups are found online, but plenty are very active offline as well and that makes sense—pitching an angel investor is still a face-to-face event. As such, it behooves you to do a Google search for the terms "angel investors," "angel investing," or "angel investor group," and the name of your city.

The Women's Investment Network (WIN) is an angel forum in Portland, Oregon, for women who are angels or would like to learn more about becoming an angel investor. The WIN looks to increase female angel investments in Oregon through "education, company presentations, and networking," and does so by facilitating relationships between female investors and entrepreneurs.

For example, the Open Angel Forum (http://openangelforum.com) is an offline group that offers entrepreneurs the chance to pitch their businesses to angels at events in various cities. According to the website, "The Open Angel Forum is dedicated to providing entrepreneurs with access to the angel investor community based solely on merit (and without fees). Additionally, we strive to build collaboration between angel investors and to inspire high-net-worth individuals to become angels."

You may have noticed the significant point, "and without fees." That is great. Beware the angel group that seems more interested in taking your money than getting you money. Different groups have different models; a fee of a few hundred is not that big a deal, and in the case of online angel networks, it is common. But just be careful out there.

Online angel groups. Maybe it is no surprise that a host of online groups have cropped up in recent years to facilitate the introduction of entrepreneur and angel. A Google search will provide you with a list to choose from, but here are a few to help you get started.

Angelsoft. Angelsoft is a business planning and funding platform that allows entrepreneurs to search through over 25,000 investors.

AngelList. "How it works: You create a pitch and select investors. . . . You can always edit the pitch or investors later. The investors review startups as they come in and ask for intros to the ones they like. The investors can't review every pitch on the site, so the AngelList admins do. If the admins find a pitch they like, they'll contact you and work with you to email the pitch to the investors you've selected." (AngelList.com.)

GoBigNetwork. There are three steps to this network: First, place your business and get it promoted throughout the site. Next, gain exposure to more than 20,000 investors. Third, meet those investors interested in your project.

Funding Universe. Recognized as one of the *Inc.* 500 fastest growing companies in the United States, Funding Universe can help with all aspects of the funding process, not just angel investing. You begin by filling out an application form and receiving an initial analysis and customized report for $99. Based on the results, you may be matched right away with funding sources, or (and this is valuable too) be told that you are not ready yet.

In that case, for a fee between $500 and $3,000 (at last check), Funding Universe can work with you on:

- Underwriting assistance
- Presentation/pitch analysis
- Incorporation assistance
- Financial help
- Business plan assistance, and so forth

Is it worth the fee? That really depends upon your situation. Getting the funding you need requires that you start, have, and/or run a real business. If you are not yet incorporated, for example, or your pitch needs work, the assistance of a pro can be invaluable.

Funded.com. Funded.com can help with all sorts of funding options, again not just angel investing. According to Mark Favre, CEO and founder of Funded.com, "I created Funded.com to help business owners trying to start or run a business while seeking funding from Venture Capital, Angel Investors, Private Equity Companies, Banks, SBA, Grants, and Individual Investors. Funded.com's services provide business owners professional support every step of the way, from concept to operation to financing and even many stages thereafter."

RaiseMeCapital.com. As with Funded.com, Raise Me Capital allows you to access not only thousands of angel investors, but other sources of funding too. With an account you get:

- An investment profile
- The ability to upload pictures of your product, business, business plan, and so forth
- Most importantly, access to the network

You get the idea. These online platforms usually charge a fee for membership (typically a few hundred dollars) and then allow you to pitch potential investors. There are no guarantees and the competition is stiff, but some people do get funding so it may be worth your while.

One last resource that you should definitely check out is *Angel Capital Education Foundation* (ACEF; go to www.angelcapitaleducation.org). Started by the highly respected Ewing Marion Kauffman Foundation and leaders of angel groups in the United States and Canada, ACEF is a non-profit organization that focuses on education and research in the field of angel investing. Note, however, that it does not provide financing, introductions, or investments. The ACEF works with the Angel Capital Association (www.angelcapitalassociation.org).

PITCHING ANGELS

Okay, so once you have lined up some angels to pitch, the question is, how do you do so most effectively? Well, it is almost like everything else you have read in this book, and have otherwise learned along the way about getting the money you need for your business: you have to be sharp, professional, a tad different, and hopefully better than the rest.

Angel investors are the most savvy businesspeople you will run across. They are smart, know their stuff down pat, and have walked the walk. You can't snow them or try to charm them and think that it will suffice. It might for Aunt Martha, but not here.

No, here you need to know your business and business plan inside out. You must understand the industry and competition, and have a clear view of the horizon. Know where you are going, why, how you plan to get there, how much it will cost, and why. On top of that, you will need to be able to pitch your business well, both in writing and in person.

Expect to be peppered with questions from the angel:

- What is your special sauce?
- Why is your solution better?
- Who is on your team, and why?

- What are your plans for dealing with the competition?
- What is your exit strategy?

Should you be fortunate enough to get funded by an angel, he or she will be part of your business, so treat your pitch as the beginning of an important relationship, because it is. Be forthright and honest. If you don't know an answer to a question, say so. Show your enthusiasm and passion.

One other important key to a successful pitch (aside from a dynamite idea, an executable plan, big sales potential, and a great team) is to be prepared—overprepared, probably. Many angel networks offer some sort of coaching before the pitch; check them out and take advantage of that if offered.

And sometimes, the angel will find *you*: Peter Cooper, founder of Feed .Informer.com (a site that offers news feeds to websites), launched his site in 2004. While it was still small, he added a PayPal button to his homepage and asked users to donate money to help him stay afloat. Within a year, he had received more than $5,000. But even better, he caught the eye of a Seattle-based angel group called Curious Office Partners. Liking what they saw, the group contacted Cooper, wanting to invest in the business. Eventually they invested around $100,000 in Cooper's site. Said one of the angels, "He had thousands of users that helped him keep his project going. I was on the lookout for a company like his."

Source: CNN.com, *"How to Find Your Angel,"* February 24, 2006.

Given that this is a challenging process, with huge gains if successful, the other question people often have is this: What can be done to increase one's chances of impressing an angel? Here are a few tips:

Look legit. Incorporate, for starters. Nothing says "novice" as much as running a business as a sole proprietorship or general partnership. In addition, have your business licenses, bank accounts, and other pro forma legal issues in order. After all, most of us are not Larry Page and Sergey Brin.

Have a good e-presence. Create a dynamite website and blog. Get active in social media *before* you ever get to the pitch room.

Have a solid business plan. In the end, other things will be more important—you, your team, the concept, the opportunity—but nevertheless, you still must have a business plan and a great executive summary.

Have a great team. I have said this several times already, but it bears repeating: few things impress angels more than having a great team. Legendary investor Guy Kawasaki of www.Alltop.com says that it is the people in the business that most interest him. Questions in his mind are: Can the team move the business forward? Can they be trusted with his money? How will they deal with adversity? What in their backgrounds prepared them for this venture? What are their strengths, and more importantly, their weaknesses? Do they know their weaknesses and can they compensate for them?

Have something substantial to offer. To the extent possible, have a prototype or some patent pending product to share. That will give you extra gravitas and reason to be taken seriously.

Know your numbers. Cold.

Impressing an angel takes hard work. But it is done every day. If they did it, so can you.

So how do you pitch? There are two types of pitches that you may encounter in this process:

1. *The elevator pitch.* You likely have heard plenty about your elevator pitch already. If you don't know, an elevator pitch is a brief statement about who you are, what your business is, and why it is special. The idea is this: If you were in an elevator with a potential angel and had just that short 30-second or so elevator ride to make a memorable impression, what is it you could say that would make a difference? That is your elevator pitch.

   Having a sharp, pithy, intriguing pitch ready to go can make all the difference between being remembered and being forgotten. You never know which simple conversation may lead to that big deal. So it is a good exercise for any entrepreneur to create their own elevator pitch. Here's how to create yours:

- *Figure out what is unique about what you are doing.* The whole idea behind a great elevator pitch is to intrigue someone enough so that they want to know more. A great elevator pitch is an ice-breaker, a commercial, and an opening salvo all rolled into one. It follows, then, that your elevator pitch must have a hook. "We are creating a new flower shop downtown" doesn't hold a candle to "We are a specialty florist that plans on franchising our unique concept—tropical flowers that bloom in the winter."
- *Make it exciting.* A superior elevator pitch increases your heart rate. It speaks to who you really are and what excites you about your business. It has integrity. What is it about your business plan that really motivates you? Incorporate that.
- *Keep it simple.* A good elevator pitch does not try to be all things to all people. Rather, it will convey a clear idea in a short amount of time. It might be a few sentences, but no more than a paragraph or so. Try to keep it under 30 seconds.
- *Write it down.* Use the aforementioned guidelines and take a stab at it. Write down your pitch, say it out loud, rewrite it, and then rewrite it again.
- *Practice, and then practice some more.* The first few times you try out your elevator pitch may be a bit uncomfortable, but it gets easier. Everything is hard before it is easy. After a while, it will become second nature to you, and when it does, you will be glad you practiced.

Remember what I always tell my daughters: "Writing is rewriting."

You never know what will come from having a great, natural elevator pitch, but you can bet whatever it is will be good.

2. *The full pitch.* If you are charming enough, or your elevator pitch is great, or your business proposal is amazing, then you should be able to schedule a full-length pitch to your angel. What will a full pitch entail?
   - *A PowerPoint presentation.* Your deck should be short, under 20 slides for sure, and maybe even no more than 10. Figure the presentation should last less than 20 minutes. Brevity is good.

- *Clarity*. Explain what the business is and why it is unique. What is the problem your business solves, what is your vision for the business, who is your customer, how will you achieve sales and at what level, who is the competition, what are your future plans, and why will you win? Yes, that is a lot to convey in 20 minutes. You can do it.
- *Benefits*. What is the opportunity for the investor?

THE TERM SHEET

Once you find an angel who is willing to invest in your business, he or she will want you to sign something called a "term sheet." This is a deal memorandum that explains the terms of the agreement. Remember the old adage: *everything is negotiable*. The terms of your deal are not set in stone, and if an angel wants to invest in your business, she wants you as much (or almost as much) as you want her. Don't fold.

For a simple angel investment (as opposed to a venture capital infusion) the term sheet should be fairly simple and it would be smart for you to have your own ready. Some of the things you will want to cover are:

- The amount of money you will receive.
- The percentage of ownership you are giving up.
- The number of shares of stock to which that corresponds.
- The number of seats on the board the angel will get.
- Other roles the investor may or may not have in the company.
- Other legal issues suggested by your attorney (inability to dilute shares, for instance).

The last thing to understand is how the angel will take his or her shares in your company. Let's say that when you started your business, you issued 1,000 shares of common stock (all of which you own). The angel may simply ask for, say, 200 shares, and thereby will become a 20 percent minority shareholder in your business. Hold tight to your remaining 80 percent, as you may need it to sell shares to your uncle, or, if you are lucky, to another angel or venture capitalist.

Angel deals typically do not close quickly. A month or two, depending upon the situation, is not uncommon. Therefore, the entire process, from the beginning of your search to the cashing of the check, can take any-where from 6 to 12 months.

Bottom Line: There are a lot of ways to find angel investors these days, but it still is a time-consuming process. Angels are out there, and they want to invest in great businesses. Give them that chance. Prepare to impress, and then prepare some more.

CHAPTER 8

Venture Capital

Essential Idea: Raise the Money by Going to the Funding Big Leagues

When it comes to getting the funding you need for your business, venture capital (VC) is the big time. It is Broadway. It is Showtime. No, getting VC funding is not easy, but it can make your business and career.

Example: In 2000, Jeffrey Bussgang was pitching his new business, Upromise, to John Doerr. Doerr is a legendary venture capitalist with the equally legendary venture capital firm Kleiner Perkins Caufield & Byers (other KPC&B investments: Google, Amazon.com, and AOL). Bussgang was motoring through his PowerPoint when, he says, Doerr stopped him suddenly and drilled down into Bussgang's numbers. Acting nonplussed (even though he was definitely plussed), Bussgang apparently answered the questions right because Upromise eventually received millions in funding from the VC firm before finally going public.

Today, Bussgang is a VC himself, the general partner at Flybridge Capital Partners, a venture capital firm with more than $500 million in assets. So Bussgang has the unique perspective of seeing the VC game from both sides of the ball. He has in fact written a great book about it—which, if you are looking for VC funding, you would be well advised to read—called *Mastering the VC Game*.

In the book, and in subsequent interviews, Bussgang has some interesting things to share about getting the money you need for your business. According to Bussgang, if you go the VC route, one key to success is your ability to show the investors that you have something unique to offer and have assembled a team capable of executing your plan. According to an interview he gave to *The Philadelphia Bulletin* newspaper (May 16, 2010), VCs "are looking for a team that works well together and has some unfair advantage in what they are bringing to the market. There are a million good ideas out there, but strong execution of the good ideas is a defining factor for success."

So it may be no surprise that in that interview, Bussgang says he looks at two things in particular when analyzing a potential VC investment: the team, and their plan. "I focus on the background of the entrepreneurs. Is it a track record of accomplishments and is it relevant to this market such that they may have a unique perspective on it?" he says. Additionally, the business plan is vital: "Either in the form of a well-done PowerPoint pitch or Word document, the business plan is important in outlining the market opportunity, providing the background of the entrepreneurs and why they are uniquely well suited for this opportunity, and providing a window into the quality of your thinking and writing."

So that should whet your appetite. If you are looking for high six-figure to seven-figure funding, then this is the chapter for you.

OVERVIEW

It is said that an entrepreneur is a person willing to take a risk with money to make money. If so, then it might also be said that a venture capitalist is an uber-entrepreneur, a super-capitalist, since a venture capitalist is a person who bets big on new business ventures that have huge upside and equal risk. Typically, they look for a 25 percent return on their investment, but they also know that that may come by investing in nine duds and one grand slam. Venture capitalist money usually goes to startups, but in this world, "startup" is a bit of a misnomer. It is not your typical,

> In the movie *The Social Network*, about the founding of Facebook, Mark Zuckerberg (as played by Jesse Eisenberg) mentions that he might be able to make a million off of Facebook. Sean Parker (co-founder of Napster and played by Justin Timberlake) retorts: "A million dollars isn't cool. You know what's cool? A billion dollars." Today, Facebook is estimated to be worth more than $50 billion. Very, very cool.

five-figure, "I dreamed a dream" sort of deal. Startups in this league are multimillion-dollar affairs.

Maybe you are thinking that a VC sounds a lot like an angel investor, and to a certain extent you would be right—both invest in businesses. But that's really where the similarities end. Angel investors are individuals who usually have interest and experience in the sorts of companies that they look to invest in and who invest their own money. Venture capitalists, on the other hand, are professional investors who run firms with partners, who invest millions in other people's money, and who are therefore looking for a significant rate of return for the firm on any sort of deal with huge upside potential.

The other thing to understand initially is that different VC firms invest in different sorts of startups. Although the high-tech, e-business startups get most of the ink, the fact is, VC money is available for almost any sort of business that has the potential to hit it big. So how do you know which firm is best for your idea? That's what the Internet is for. As discussed in the following pages, different partners and different firms have different areas of interest and sweet spots. You will discover that there are thousands of VC firms around the United States from which to choose.

But before you get there, you need to start down the right path.

THE FUNDING PROCESS

Getting to the place where you can seek VC money is no easy feat. And once you are there, you enter into a rarefied, specialized business world with a nomenclature all its own. For instance, in this world the money you got from your parents is not called "the bank of mom and dad"; rather it is "seed round" funding. The point where an angel may wish to invest in your business is called, not surprisingly, the "angel round" of funding.

After that, you may be ready for even more funding, for "series" funding. You know you are there if your business, while successful, still requires even more money for the idea to really fly. It could be for marketing, or product development, or hiring staff to ramp up, or inventory—anything, really. Whatever the case, at that point, venture capital money is needed. Yes, there are those few businesses that get VC money far earlier than this, that go from seed round to VC round, but they are more the exception than the rule. The VC round has several subrounds.

The Series A Round. If a VC firm likes the business, it will offer the entrepreneurs a "term sheet" (see Chapter 7, "Angel Investors"). The term sheet will outline the terms of any eventual deal and will lock the startup up; that is, while the VC does its due diligence and investigates the business and opportunity, the entrepreneurs are forbidden from pitching to any additional VC firms.

Once the due diligence is completed (one to two months) and the deal is a go, the venture capital firm will value the business. This is necessary since everyone needs to know how much of the business the VC firm is getting for its investment. Investing $1 million in a business worth $2 million (50 percent) is very different than if the business is worth $10 million (10 percent). Business valuation is a tricky matter and, although beggars can't be choosers, it would nevertheless be smart to have your own valuation ready.

Here, then, is where the fun starts. If the business is worth $4 million and the VCs want to invest $1 million, they become 25 percent stakeholders (unless more shares are issued), and will have several seats on the board and likely management authority as well. The business then gets a lump sum of money (or possibly in stages) and gets to work. Its job is to use the money to grow the business so that the business becomes even more valuable and therefore eligible for the Series B round.

According to venture capitalist Lee Hower, cofounder and partner of NextView Ventures (and former entrepreneur at LinkedIn and PayPal), "Entrepreneurs who succeed in raising a first round of VC funding have essentially established plausibility of three things: Suitable market opportunity, some ability to differentiate, and a core team's ability to get it launched" (www.agilevc.com).

The Series B Round. This is the second round of VC funding. According to Lee Hower at www.agilevc.com, the key to getting funding at this stage is the ability to prove one's concept:

> *Proving a concept means different things in different sorts of industry sectors. For a consumer-facing company it generally means product launch with some compelling, if early, data on usage and often even initial revenue. For companies with B2B software business models, it usually means an initial set of customer wins. It might be design milestones for a semiconductor startup, or clinical*

trial data for a life sciences startup. The point is that raising a second round of VC financing almost always means that a company had proven its vision at least on a limited scale.

Guy Kawasaki is a well-known Silicon Valley VC, writer, and entrepreneur. Here is Guy's list of the "top lies of venture capitalists":

1. "I liked your company, but my partners didn't." What the sponsor is trying to get the entrepreneur to believe is that he's the good guy, the smart guy; the "others" didn't, so don't blame him. This is a cop-out; it's not that the other partners didn't like the deal as much as the sponsor wasn't a true believer. A true believer would get it done.
2. "If you get [another VC] to take the lead, we will follow." In other words, once the entrepreneur doesn't need the money, the venture capitalist would be happy to give him some more.
3. "Show us some traction, and we'll invest." This lie translates to, "I don't believe your story, but if you can prove it by achieving significant revenue, then you might convince me."
4. "We're investing in your team." This is an incomplete statement. What he or she is saying is, "We're investing in your team as long as things are going well, but if they go bad we will fire your ass because no one is indispensable."

Source: blog.guykawasaki.com.

Series C Funding. Hower says that at this stage, the startups "have generally demonstrated certainty in their business at moderate scale. This could mean a clear track record of revenue growth, possibly even reaching breakeven or beyond."

Series D/Prepublic Funding. This is the last stage of the VC funding process. The point here is to get ready to go public (see next chapter, *"The Initial Public Offering (IPO)"*).

There is more than one type of stock in a business. For the sake of simplicity, think of stock as having two tiers. The basic sort of stock is called "common" stock. The other is more important. It is called "preferred" stock. It is preferred because it gets extra rights, such as being paid first in any dissolution, veto power, and antidilution provisions. Venture capitalists like to get preferred shares in the company.

FINDING VENTURE CAPITALISTS

Okay, so now that you know how VCs work and what VC money looks like and costs, the question (as always, it seems) is how do you find them? And again, as with angels, the answer is that a personal introduction works best. There are some startups that get funded by cold-calling or cold-e-mailing a VC or VC firm, but it occurs far less often that you would like. The response rate to this sort of plan is, sadly, near zero.

So your best bet is to locate the VC and firm that is in the proverbial sweet spot for your business, and then work to get introduced to that VC. There are several ways to do this. You start by doing your online research about the different VC firms in your area (most VCs like to invest in projects within driving distance). There are several portal websites that list different VC firms, such as:

- Gaebler.com: Lists VC firms by state.
- The Funded.com: Also lists VC firms.
- PE Data Center: For a fee, you can get access to an interactive database that includes names of partners, deal terms, and investment history.
- VCPro Database: A downloadable VC and private equity directory with profiles of over 4,000 venture capital firms worldwide.
- FundingPost.com: Not only does Funding Post list over 7,000 angel investors and VCs, but it has showcase events across the country.
- The National Venture Capital Association's Online Membership Directory: This database offers contact information and investment preferences (www.nvca.org).

Once you have located some VC firms that best fit the profile of your business, then you should try to narrow your search down even further and find the partners in those firms who seem most likely to be receptive to your business. Try to figure out a way to get to meet them or get an introduction. This is where LinkedIn may come in handy. By first locating the right VCs for your business, and then finding any possible connections you may have to them, with LinkedIn it is possible to meet the people you need to know.

What if you have no connection to the VC of your choice? What do you do? Consider these options:

- Hire a corporate attorney with connections to the VC world and get an introduction that way.
- If you graduated from a college with a good business department, see if the head of the department can make some introductions.
- Have a CEO of a well-known company make an introduction.
- If all else fails, try a short, clever email to the VC.

Once you find that magical VC, it is time to set up a meeting. Remember this too: You have only one chance to make a great first impression. The VC world is one that relies heavily on first impressions, and not only that, but it is a small club. If you don't impress that first VC, if he or she passes, that can taint you as you shop your business to other VCs. It's a small club.

The time to approach a VC, therefore, is only when you are very ready. You need to have a team, plan, hot idea, and business in place. Again, some of this might be missing, but essentially these guys get pitched a lot—heck, they get pitched for a living—so you have to be ready to knock it out of the park.

THE PITCH

There really are two sorts of pitches, and they are similar to the pitches discussed earlier in the chapter on angel investors. Re-read that chapter. In addition, previously I mentioned two well-known VCs who had advice on VC funding—Guy Kawasaki and Jeffrey Bussgang. Both have something valuable to add here as well.

When it comes to the pitch, Kawasaki says that entrepreneurs should try to stick to what he calls the "10-20-30" rule:

- The PowerPoint presentation should be 10 slides.
- The slides enable you to speak for 20 minutes.
- Thus, you should use a font size that is no smaller than 30 points.

The reasoning behind this rule is that it forces you to be succinct and to the point. Kawasaki even suggests how you should organize your slides:

1. Contact info/title
2. The problem
3. Your solution
4. Business model/how you plan on making money
5. Underlying magic—patents, trademarks, something new, your unique value proposition
6. Marketing
7. Sales
8. Competition—what can you do that they cannot?
9. The team
10. Conclusion

It may be hard to get everything you want to say into 10 slides and 20 minutes, but his point is well taken. A 60-slide PowerPoint deck that you hope to use for an hour will get tuned out, pronto.

Similarly, Jeffrey Bussgang has some valuable insights with regard to the sorts of questions you should expect from the VC in an article from *Inc.* magazine (May 1, 2010), such as:

- "Why are you uniquely positioned to succeed?"
- "Why couldn't three people from Bangalore who have the same idea outexecute you?"
- "How are you going to make me money?"

Bussgang says that getting peppered with questions is a good thing. "The more probing the VC is, the more interested he probably is in what you're doing."

Your job is to be enthusiastic, honest, smart, savvy, and articulate. Make sure your numbers crunch. Have something unique and better to offer.

Bottom Line: Venture capitalists are professional investors, so approach them only when you are ready to play in the big leagues. When you are, make yours a pitch that clearly demonstrates that you can make the VC a lot of money. If you do that, you will knock it out of the park.

CHAPTER 9

The Initial Public Offering (IPO)

Essential Idea: Take Your Private Company Public by Selling Shares on the Open Market

Remember the dot-com era? It was a freewheeling, big-spending, high-flying time where fortunes were made and lost as companies competed to be the latest and greatest Internet sensation. For those businesses, the mountaintop was the IPO—the initial public offering. Getting to the place where a startup would go public meant that all of those years (or months, as it were) and risks paid off in one day when the founders became instant millionaires and savvy VCs saw their net worth net more.

Take, for example, Pets.com. If you don't remember the name, you probably remember its mascot, the Pets.com dog sock puppet. The talking sock puppet became a cultural icon in the year 2000. Interviewed on the *Today* show by Matt Lauer and the star of its own Super Bowl commercial, the dog sock puppet even became a float in the Macy's Thanksgiving Day Parade. One would think that with publicity like that, Pets.com was destined for a huge IPO and a booming business.

You would be only half right.

It turns out that the marketing wizards at Pets.com were indeed marketing wizards. But marketing is only one piece of a successful business, and certainly not enough in and of itself to carry things forward over the long haul. There are lots of other moving parts to a business that have to work for it to be successful: a valid idea, a great team, know-how, smart pricing, and much more. For Pets.com, the problem was that it wasn't actually a great idea. Who really wants to buy pet food, kitty litter, or flea spray online and wait a few days for delivery? Usually you need those things when you need them, not in a few days.

But folks hadn't yet realized that when Pets.com went public on February 11, 2000. That day the company raised an astounding $82.5 million by selling shares of the company to the public. The stock closed at more than $11 a share, which is all the more astonishing given that Pets.com had not even come close to turning a profit yet. Indeed, the company was apparently selling products at prices approximately 27 percent *below* cost. Of course, no business can sustain an economic model like that for long, not even one with a famous sock as its mascot.

Nine months after its $82.5 million IPO, Pets.com was out of business. Share price on the last day: 19 cents.

In the year leading up to its IPO, Pets.com earned $619,000 in revenues. It spent $11.8 million on advertising.

OVERVIEW

Okay, so let's say that you have created a very cool company and that, unlike Pets.com, it is a viable business. Maybe you went through some or all of the financing rounds mentioned in previous chapters—friends and family, SBA loans, angel investors, and even some VC money. So now you have reached the pinnacle, prompting the question: Is it time to go public? To even get to that point is an amazing accomplishment that very few businesses aspire to, let alone reach.

Why would a private company want to go the IPO route and become a publicly traded company? After all, there are definite benefits to remaining private. There are fewer people to be accountable to and the strict SEC (securities) laws that regulate publicly traded companies are not applicable to privately held businesses. Consider that in 2011, Facebook still had not become a public company because founder and CEO Mark Zuckerberg found numerous benefits to remaining private. (That said, Facebook also did not need the money that an IPO can generate.)

But despite the benefits that may come with being privately held, the first and main reason a company would want to go public is money. By selling shares of stock in the company to the public, the business can generate millions of dollars.

Beyond that, there are some additional motivations for going public:

- Increased exposure
- Status
- Diversifying the financial base of the company
- Generating cash for the owners

How does one actually take a private business public, if that is the plan? The basic five-step IPO process looks like this:

1. Hire investment bankers to facilitate the undertaking.
2. Create and submit the SEC registration documents.
3. Go on the "road show."
4. Value the selling price of the shares that will be issued.
5. Sell the shares.

Let's look at each step a little more closely.

1. CHOOSE AN INVESTMENT BANKER AND OTHER PROFESSIONALS

Once a company's management has made the decision to seek an initial public offering, the next step is to find an investment bank or banks to underwrite the process. "Underwriting" is the process by which the bankers raise capital from investors on behalf of the company. In essence, the underwriter agrees to presell the stock to institutional investors before the shares actually hit the open market. In this sense, "underwriting" hearkens back to the original definition of the word whereby people would write their name under the amount of risk they were willing to assume.

Investment banks may underwrite an IPO on either a "best effort" or a "firm commitment" basis. "Best effort" is exactly what it sounds like— the underwriting bank promises only to give its best effort. It may or may not raise the capital necessary and presell enough shares to go public. A "firm commitment" deal, however, is one where the underwriters actually agree to purchase shares of the business—at a discount, of course. The bankers then set about reselling these shares to institutional investors and the general public. Compared to a firm commitment, a best effort deal should be a sign that the bank may have some misgivings about the IPO.

So while the process of hiring an investment banker is probably very new to you, and clearly crucial to the success of the IPO, it is also not unlike hiring any other professional: You need to find a firm you trust, one that believes in your business, people with whom you communicate well, and a group with whom the personalities involved mesh. The bankers should also know your industry well so as to help value your company properly.

The actual process of finding and securing an investment banker requires that you meet and greet them. Not surprisingly, then, this process is also sometimes called "the beauty contest." But make no mistake about it, it is serious business. Your investment banking firm will make or break your IPO. Have these bankers handled similar IPOs before, and if so, how successful were they? What are they like to work with? Do your due diligence and pick a winner.

> Investment bankers include the biggest names in the banking business, such as Bank of America, Citigroup, Chase, Credit Suisse, Deutsche Bank, and Goldman Sachs.

Similarly, as the legal hoops the company must jump through are both numerous and complicated, it is vital that you line up a law firm that is experienced in the IPO process. Hiring established law firms with extensive work in the securities field is essential to IPO success.

2. CREATE AND SUBMIT THE REGISTRATION DOCUMENTS

Initial public offerings are regulated by the federal government. Thus, to proceed with an IPO, a company must submit a registration statement to the SEC. This is no pro forma document; it must fully, accurately, and carefully disclose the following:

- The history of the business's formation, management, prospects, and strengths.
- An explanation of how the company plans on using the proceeds of the IPO.
- Risk factors associated with the business.
- A history of all directors, officers, and principal shareholders.
- Legal proceedings the company is involved in.
- Audited books.
- Copies of relevant corporate documents.

> The SEC disclosure document is also at various times called the prospectus, the red herring prospectus, and the S-1 filing.

Once all of these documents have been submitted to the SEC, a several-month review process is undertaken. During this time the company and its investment bankers can discuss the IPO with potential buyers.

3. GO ON THE ROAD SHOW

Now the fun begins (or not, depending upon your perspective). The road show is a multicity tour whereby the company's management meets with prospective investors to gauge interest in buying shares of the company when it goes public. If you have ever followed an IPO, you will recall that shares are first sold to institutional investors before they become available on the open market for the general public. The road show is what precedes that.

If you think there might be a lot of pressure on the management team during this process, you would be correct. The team has to woo and impress these institutional investors (e.g., banks, mutual funds, insurance companies, retirement funds, etc.) such that they will want to purchase a significant percentage of the shares when they hit the market.

4. VALUE THE SHARES

At some point after the completion of the road show, the final prospectus will be distributed to various investors. It is at this point, before the offering date, that the company and its investment bankers meet to decide how many shares to sell and at what price per share.

Deciding on a share price is a tricky business; many things come into play in this calculation, including the demand for a piece of this company, the state of the market, the general economy, the need for the initial investors to see their investment increase, and the ability of the company to raise the capital it seeks.

The basic idea is to price the stock just below where the stock is expected to trade once it hits the market. The purpose of this underpricing is to create buzz and increase sales once the stock hits the open market. But if the share price is set too low, the company will leave money on the table, as the IPO will not generate as much as it could for the business. If the share price is set too high, potential buyers will be turned off. So, like Goldilocks's porridge, the share price must be just right.

Note that these initial prices are not set in stone. An IPO that is hot will see its offering price rise before the initial offering. The opposite can happen as well. In the rare case, an IPO may be canceled due to lack of interest (and not before the company has spent maybe hundreds of thousands of dollars hiring banks and lawyers and going through the due diligence process).

Underpricing a stock in an IPO has significant consequences. Take the case of TheGlobe.com. One of the late 1990s dot-com era IPOs, the company's stock (underwritten by the now-defunct Bear Stearns) was priced at only $9 a share. On the first day of trading it skyrocketed to $97, but it quickly dropped to $63 as the institutional investors sought to profit immediately from the run-up since they had bought it around the $9 mark. Similarly, although TheGlobe.com did raise $30 million, had its stock been more accurately valued—in the mid-$60s, for example—it is estimated that it would have received about $200 million from its IPO.

Once the price is set, and the day before the IPO, the company will sell the agreed-upon shares to the underwriters and institutional investors.

5. SELL, SELL, SELL!

On the day of the IPO, the exchange, whether it be the NASDAQ or the New York Stock Exchange (NYSE), will often have a ceremony to commemorate the event. Money from the institutional investors will go to the corporation, roughly equating to 92 percent of the agreed-upon value of the stock. The other 8 percent will go as commissions to lawyers, bankers, and accountants. The money the company receives that first day of the IPO is all it will see from the event; thereafter, all trading is done between investors in the stock market.

Bottom Line: The IPO is the pinnacle of money generation for a new company. It is a steep and rare hill to climb, and one that can make you rich.

Using Your Own Resources

CHAPTER 10

Factoring

Essential Idea: Raise Money by Selling Your Accounts Receivable

Let's say that Bobblehead Co. makes custom wooden bobbleheads that it wholesales for $10 each. One day, Bobblehead Co. gets a large order for 5,000 bobbleheads from e-Commerce Corp. Bobblehead spends a few weeks, makes the bobbleheads, and delivers them to e-Commerce Corp. on June 1. Bobblehead is now owed $50,000.

That same day, Bobblehead gets another large order, this time from Super Co. The problem is that, because e-Commerce Corp. has a policy of paying its bills net 30, Bobblehead Co. has not received the $50,000 it is owed and therefore, it does not have the capital on hand that it needs to buy the materials to fulfill its order for Super Co. on time. If e-Commerce Corp. does not pay Bobblehead for another 30 days, Bobblehead will lose its super sale to Super Co.

What to do?

Factoring to the rescue! Factoring is the selling of a business's accounts receivable to a third party in order to obtain immediate funding. Often the money can be received within 24 to 48 hours. In this case, Bobblehead Co. can sell to Factoring Co. the $50,000 it is owed from e-Commerce Corp. and get paid right away. It will then have enough money to fulfill its order to Super Co. (and even better, you won't have to read any more silly made-up company names)!

Whereas factoring was once a sort of exotic idea, these days it is a commonplace way for businesses of all kinds to get the capital they need without having to apply for a bank loan or sell a piece of the company to an investor. Literally billions of dollars in accounts receivable are factored every year.

UNDERSTANDING THE PLAYERS AND TERMS

Even though the idea of factoring is easy to understand—you are owed money so you sell that "asset" to someone else—factoring is still a specialized way of getting money. It has its own language. The following are the terms you need to know:

Client. You (presumably). The company that is owed money on an invoice.

Account debtor. Your client or customer. The one who owes you money.

Accounts receivable. Money owed to you, generally due within 90 days or less.

Factor. The company that is willing to buy the accounts receivable so as to provide businesses with operating capital.

Advance rate. The amount of money, expressed as a percentage less than the 100 percent you are owed by a customer. This is the amount the factor will advance you on the invoice.

Verification. This is the process whereby the factor verifies that you have in fact provided a product or service for a customer and that the customer plans on paying the invoice.

Discount fee. The fee that the factor will charge you for the service. Let's say that the factor pays you a 98 percent advance rate. The other 2 percent is the discount fee. The discount fee is determined by:
- The amount of the invoice.
- The perceived risk involved.
- How long it is expected to take to collect the funds.
- The creditworthiness of your customer (not you, since you do not owe the money; your customer does).

Reserve. A deposit maintained by the factor. It is used to protect the factor against nonpayment should a dispute arise between the client and its customer. The reserve is sent to the client only after the customer has paid the factor the amount owed on the invoice.

As should be obvious, the client does not get 100 cents on the dollar when using factoring. Not only must it pay a percentage of the accounts receivable to the factor, but a reserve is also retained and not received until much later.

> Factoring facts: In the United States, the South is the region where factoring is the most predominant, accounting for 25 percent of all factoring contracts. By far, the worst year in recent memory for factoring was 2001. In 2010, factoring was a $150 billion a year industry.

FACTORING FACTORS

Obviously, factoring is not an idea that works for most startups, because consistent accounts receivable must be in the pipeline for a factor to be interested. But for those more established companies that do have money owed to them every month, factoring can be a great solution. It can provide immediate working capital for inventory, payroll, improved facilities, projects, anything.

In return for that almost-instant cash, you must be willing to give up some of the money you are owed to the factor, and also be willing to have the company whose invoice you are selling learn of the sale; it will be paying the invoice to the factor and not to you.

Another nice thing about factoring is that it is a relatively easy and quick process, especially in comparison to, say, getting a bank loan. Indeed, the factor cares little about your creditworthiness and is really only concerned about the payment history of your customer. If your customer pays in full and on time, you are in business. Usually all the factor needs from you is proof that all services are complete or that all products have been delivered as promised. Once you show that, selling your invoice on that deal should be a breeze.

> Factoring is ancient. The earliest known account of factoring is in Babylonia's Code of Hammurabi, which dealt with, among other things, the trade practices of merchants, their agents, and how to properly deal with trade credits.

Factoring makes sense for a lot of different businesses. For example, if your cash flow varies greatly from month to month—maybe it is a seasonal business—factoring could be a boon for you. It has several benefits:

- Evens out cash flow throughout the year.
- Gives you steady working capital.
- Covers short-term cash crunches.
- Greatly decreases the time from when an order is delivered to when the invoice is paid.
- Reduces some invoicing issues as the factor will make sure that it gets paid.

Despite all of the upside benefits of factoring, the process is not without its risk and downsides, including:

- Lost opportunity. By giving up money later for cash now, a business makes less than it otherwise would. What could you do with that extra money you will be paying to the factor? That is called the "lost opportunity cost" and should be considered.
- It can be a crutch. Factoring can be a sort of financial crutch, allowing you to put off that day when you can cover your own nut. By bearing down with some frugality, it is possible that you could get through a short-term cash crunch long enough to get paid and even out the cycle on your own.
- There is a chance that the client does not pay the factor. In that case, the factor will come after you for the money, which you may or may not have.
- It is expensive. As indicated, factor rates vary depending upon the circumstances. You may get 85 percent of your invoice; you may get 98 percent.

- There is a chance that you and your client may get into a dispute about the amount owed or the product they received. That puts the factor in the middle and effectively ends your relationship with the factoring company.
- There may be an effect on your clients. Will your customers think your business is in trouble because you hired a factor? That is, why are you unable to wait 60 days to get paid? What does that say about your business? It may say nothing, but it is something to consider.
- A related issue has to do with your reputation in the community at large since the old belief was that factoring is for businesses that were poor credit risks and could not get a bank loan. That is less true these days, but again, it is something to be aware of.

> Because factoring can be expensive—you may sell the invoice for as little as 85 percent of its value, plus fees—you might want to consider this creative alternative: You can give your own customers a discount for paying your invoice quickly. What about a 5 percent discount for paying within 30 days and a 10 percent discount for paying within two weeks of receiving the invoice? Paying 10 percent beats paying a factor 15 percent.

WHERE AND HOW TO FIND FACTORING COMPANIES

If you decide that you would like to explore the factoring potential of your business, finding a factor is easy. Is really is a matter of doing an Internet search and then doing your homework on the companies you find to make sure they are legitimate and good to work with. One nice thing about this Internet age we live in is that you do not necessarily need to find a factor in your city. Factoring is easily something that can be done virtually.

Once you find a factoring company with the potential to meet your needs, here are the questions you should ask:

- What are the basic fees? How much of your invoice will you be paid and what percentage is their fee?

- What are the extra, hidden fees in the contract? For example, is there an initiation fee, a due diligence fee, or a late invoice fee?
- What is the reputation of the company? How long have they been around? Who are their clients? What do people say about them? Do people like working with this company? Are they fair and flexible or rigid and dogmatic?

DEALING WITH INTERNATIONAL GOODS

In this increasingly interconnected global "e-conomy" we live in, ever more small businesses are involved in international trade and commerce. Either they are selling their goods through their website to international customers or they are sourcing products overseas and shipping them here for resale. The latter scenario is one where factoring may come into play too.

A problem these small businesses have is that, even if they have a large order for goods they are bringing in from, say, China, selling that receivable (or even getting a loan against it) is often next to impossible before the goods are delivered to their domestic customer. Domestic banks are reluctant to lend on goods in transit, as are factoring companies. That leaves the small businesses with valuable inventory and accounts receivable against which they cannot borrow critical capital. What do you do?

Well, where there is a need, there is usually an innovative company that will look to fill that market gap. That is the case here. If you routinely deal with international shipments, orders, and invoices, you should know about a program offered by UPS Capital (a division of United Parcel Service). This program offers a unique solution that enables businesses to finance in-transit shipments of inventories sourced from international suppliers, as well as inventory housed overseas. UPS Capital will lend on the value of in-transit and warehoused inventory *if* UPS manages the in-transit shipments or if the inventory is warehoused in UPS facilities. Because UPS Capital knows exactly where all of the goods being financed are at any given time, it can safely lend you money on that inventory.

Bottom Line: Factoring can be a smart way to eliminate cash-flow shortages and get an immediate infusion of capital.

CHAPTER 11

Retirement Accounts

Essential Idea:
Use Your Retirement Funds

Now here is a story from a bygone era, from *Fortune Small Business Magazine* ("Take Charge of Your IRA," May 21, 2007):

> *Last November, Dave Hanrahan, 37, of Vineland, NJ, decided to try something different to improve the returns in his retirement account. Rather than putting his money into the latest hot stock or biotech fund, Hanrahan used $60,000 in his self-directed IRA to purchase a small residential building lot. Thirty days later he flipped it for a tidy profit.*
>
> *Ordinarily such a move would result in a capital gains tax. But because the property was held by his IRA, Hanrahan will owe no tax on the gain until decades from now when he starts taking distributions on the account. "Otherwise I would have paid about 30 percent tax on the sale," he says.*

This story is interesting on a couple of different levels. The first, of course, is that the gentleman in question not only speculated with his retirement account to buy real estate, but flipped it for "a tidy profit" in 30 days. The good old days, indeed. The second—and for our purposes—more relevant issue is that he was able to safely use his individual retirement account (IRA) for a business venture and did so without penalty. That this can be done should be welcome news.

Indeed, if you are considering using your retirement account to fund your business, whether the fund is an IRA or a 401(k), the most important thing in the process is to minimize the risks and penalties to the extent possible.

RISKS

I almost need not say what the biggest risk here is, but I will anyway because it bears repeating: *This is your retirement fund!* You simply must be very sure of your course and very committed to its execution if you plan on using this nest egg to finance your business. While that is the sort of passion it takes to become a successful entrepreneur, you must still be smart and prudent as you proceed. After all, the days of investing $60,000 in a real estate deal and flipping it for a profit in 30 days are long gone.

There are more and less risky ways to use your retirement money to fund a business; it all depends on your goals, situation, and the type of retirement account you have. We will examine them all, but just remember: less risky is better.

> "Until one is committed, there is hesitancy, the chance to draw back, always ineffectiveness. Concerning all acts of initiative (and creation), there is one elementary truth the ignorance of which kills countless ideas and splendid plans: that the moment one definitely commits oneself, the providence moves too. A whole stream of events issues from the decision, raising in one's favor all manner of unforeseen incidents, meetings and material assistance, which no man could have dreamt would have come his way. I learned a deep respect for one of Goethe's couplets:
>
> *Whatever you can do or dream you can, begin it.*
> *Boldness has genius, power and magic in it!"*
>
> Source: W. H. Murray, *The Scottish Himalayan Expedition*, 1951.

USING YOUR INDIVIDUAL RETIREMENT ACCOUNT (IRA)

Take the money and run. Maybe you are thinking that there is only one way to use your IRA for your business: namely, withdraw the funds, take the penalty, and pay the tax due. Fortunately, that is not the only way, and not even close to the best way, but since it is a well-known way, let's examine it first.

(Caveat: There are all sorts of different IRAs and they have different rules—traditional IRAs, SEP IRAs, Roth IRAs, and so on. Before doing anything, check with your own financial adviser to see what rules apply to your account. In this section, we are talking *generally* about IRAs.)

The analysis you need to engage in is this: What is the likelihood that you will generate more money with your new business than with your old IRA, and is it worth taking the chance that you may lose your retirement account altogether?

Example: Let's say that you decide to withdraw $100,000 from your IRA and you are not yet $59\frac{1}{2}$ years old so you will have to pay the penalty. Let's further assume that you earn 5 percent on this account—$5,000 yearly. By taking the money out of the account early, you will pay $10,000 in penalties, and, depending upon your tax bracket, maybe something like $30,000 in taxes. You will therefore have but $60,000 left to invest in your business. The question then is, how much can you expect to earn from this business? If your idea is the winner you believe it to be, it is a lot more than the $5,000 you were earning yearly in the IRA. But if it doesn't work, you are out $100,000 and a lot of peace of mind. It's a tough call.

Fortunately, this plan of having your money and paying taxes on it too is not the only way to use your IRA to fund your business. The following are some less risky ways:

Take the money and get a deduction. In this scenario, you offset the money you take out of your IRA with a corresponding tax deduction for the expenses the money will go toward. Example: You withdraw $20,000 from your IRA and spend it on business expenses. Those expenses are tax deductible, of course. As such, the deduction should help offset the taxes owed for the withdrawal. Note that you will still have to pay the 10 percent penalty if you are not yet $59\frac{1}{2}$.

Take a short-term, interest-free loan from your IRA. This nifty (but limited) trick is the one used by the real estate investor at the beginning of this chapter. The IRS laws allow you to borrow your IRA money for up to 60 days penalty-free. That means you could take out $10,000 and, if you repay it within two months (not later; the rules are strict), you will incur no penalty.

One downside to this, aside from the limited time you can use it, is that you will not be able to access all of the money you want because a portion is held in reserve for the possible payment of taxes (should you be late or default). How much? Try 10 to 30 percent.

If the previous chapter on factoring makes sense for your business, you may want to consider the 60-day, interest-free IRA loan instead, as you will not have to pay any fees to a factor this way.

Maybe you are thinking that you could take out a series of back-to-back interest-free IRA loans, using one to pay another. That is, could you borrow $10,000 from one IRA account for 59 days and then $10,000 from another one on day 59 and pay the first one back, effectively giving you a recurring loan? Possibly. Note, however, that you would need different IRA accounts to do this and the assistance of a lawyer or tax professional to make sure you are doing everything properly and legally.

Invest through your IRA. This process is more complicated. As you may know, it is possible to self-direct investments directly into stocks in your IRA, so another option is this: In conjunction with an attorney, you could set up a corporation and issue shares of stock. You then use your IRA funds to buy those shares. Your IRA will then own part of your corporation. The money you receive from the stock purchase can then be used in your business and profits must go proportionally back to the IRA. Again, check with a tax attorney and financial planner before going this route.

If all of this talk about penalties and taxes gives you heartburn, then consider the beauty of a Roth IRA. With a Roth IRA, you can withdraw your contributions *at any time* before the age of $59\frac{1}{2}$—tax and penalty free! What you cannot do without garnering a penalty is withdraw the earnings on those contributions, but still . . .

USING YOUR 401(K)

Of course, all of the caveats relating to tapping your IRA apply equally well here: Using your retirement funds to invest in a risky entrepreneurial venture should be a choice of last resort. It is not recommended. But yes, people do it, and you can too; just work to reduce the risk to the extent possible.

Here are your options:

Withdraw the money. As with an IRA, the same rules apply here. If you withdraw the money from your 401(k) before the age of $59\frac{1}{2}$, you will have to pay a 10 percent penalty, as well as all taxes that have been deferred. Not a great plan.

Take out a loan against the account. Again, and not surprisingly, the rules are similar to those for an IRA, but with some significant differences. There are two ways to take out a 401(k) loan:

1. Roll it over into your new business. Because your old employer will not administer your 401(k) since you (presumably) no longer work there, you will need to incorporate a new business. The old 401(k) will become your retirement account in the new business. Once that happens, you can take out a loan against your new business's new 401(k).

   The catch is that you can borrow only $50,000, or 50 percent of the account, whichever is less. Moreover, legally, you will need to repay the loan within five years, quarterly, and at a somewhat hefty interest rate.

2. Probably the better way is what is sometimes called a ROBS loan, and no, that does not stand for robbing Peter to pay Paul. A ROBS loan stands for Rollovers as Business Startups.

   Here, you would hire a company to start and administer a new 401(k) plan for your new business, funded by your old 401(k). The retirement fund then buys shares in the new business and thus the business becomes the investment portfolio of the 401(k) plan. The beauty of this plan is that there are no taxes or penalties for using the 401(k) funds for your business. And you are investing in your own business.

> Not surprisingly, the IRS closely scrutinizes the early withdrawal of a 401(k) for a ROBS loan. The fear is that the company is not really legitimate and is being used or created only to sidestep IRS regulations. Be prepared to document your ROBS loan.

Utilize a Roth 401(k). Just as with a Roth IRA, contributions made into a Roth 401(k) are more easily accessed, with fewer penalties and complications, than with a traditional 401(k).

Bottom Line: Using retirement funds to start or grow a business can be a very risky venture. It can be done, but usually it is smarter to seek out alternative methods before going this way. If you do decide to use this method, utilizing the assistance of a lawyer, financial planner, or tax professional is important.

SECTION III

Other Options

CHAPTER 12

Government Options

Essential Idea: Check Out a Variety of Government-Backed Programs to Get Funded

Time magazine named it one of its Best Inventions of the Year ("Bright Idea," November 13, 2006):

> *Identifying drunk drivers could get a lot quicker and easier after a new infrared alcohol test—developed by an Albuquerque, NM, start-up—is launched next year. Using the fact that body tissue with alcohol in it absorbs more light than normal tissue, the device detects alcohol levels by shining infrared light on the subject's skin and analyzing tissue based on how it reflects that light. The test (which doesn't have an official name yet) takes 60 sec. to produce results vs. 20 min. for a Breathalyzer test and days for a standard blood test. Inventor: TruTouch Technologies.*

This privately held company has created a terrific product that has applications in fields as diverse as medical diagnosing, law enforcement, and workplace and industrial safety. It is a hit because, aside from the reasons above, no user training is required, and results are catalogued automatically.

TruTouch Technologies raised the money to create its invention, partially through government grants, in two rounds.

In the first round, TruTouch raised $244,479 to help develop the technology. The grant came from the Qualifying Therapeutic Discovery Project (QTDP), administered under section 48D of the Internal Revenue Code and the IRS. This program offered grants to businesses that demonstrated the potential to develop "new therapies to treat chronic conditions or unmet medical needs, reducing long-term health care costs in the United States." (www.trutouchtechnologies.com.)

Said Dr. Trent Ridder, CTO of TruTouch, on the TruTouch website, the grant "recognizes our commitment to reducing the devastating medical costs caused by alcohol related accidents and injuries. [It] will help advance the commercialization of our TruTouch intoxication detection systems that are already enjoying success in the law enforcement, oil and drilling, military, and transportation markets."

In the second round, TruTouch received a $438,000 grant to "accelerate the development" of its cutting-edge technology. As opposed to the first grant, this one was administered by the United States Army Medical Research and Materiel Command (USAMRMC).

The point of sharing this story is twofold:

1. It proves that yes, there are some of those magic government grants out there that we all hear about.
2. Hopefully, the story also illustrates that such grants are very specific and often very technical in nature.

The fact is, while there is indeed some limited grant money available to business (as discussed later), it is definitely not for startups, and also is hard to get. For the most part, all of that "free government money to start a business" stuff we hear about is just so much baloney. Yes, there is government help out there for businesses, but the vast majority of it comes in the form of government loans and expertise.

As the federal website Grants.gov says, "We have all seen them; late night infomercials, websites, and reference guides, advertising 'millions in free money.' Don't believe the hype! Although there are many grants on Grants.gov, few of them are available to individuals and none of them are available for personal financial assistance."

With that qualification, and since there are some grants out there and grants are one of the funding areas of most interest to entrepreneurs, in this chapter we will start by looking at obtaining federal and state grants, and then go on to the more realistic option of federal, state, and community loans.

FEDERAL GRANTS

In this context, a grant is an award of financial assistance from a government agency. It is given to a company to further some public policy objective or other public purpose. In the case of TruTech, for instance, the grants received were to help reduce health care costs by battling alcohol-related accidents and injuries.

For a small business to be eligible for a federal grant, it must first meet the size requirement standards as set forth by the SBA:

- At most, 500 employees for the majority of manufacturing and mining industries.
- At most, 100 employees for all wholesale trade industries.
- No more than $6 million in revenue for most retail and service industries.
- No more than $28.5 million in revenue for most general and heavy construction industries.
- $12 million in revenue max for all special trade contractors.
- $0.75 million maximum revenue for most agricultural industries.

Federal government grants are administered by the many and various agencies of the government and are given out for specific purposes to further specific goals in each agency. Here are a few examples:

- The US Department of Agriculture awards a grant of up to $75,000 to "expand, or assist in the improvement and expansion of, domestic farmers markets, roadside stands, community-supported agriculture programs, and other direct producer-to-consumer market opportunities." (USDA.gov.)
- The Department of Commerce offers a three-year grant of up to $400,000 "to provide electronic and one-on-one business assistance to rapid growth potential minority-owned businesses. Eligible beneficiaries of this program

have been designated as African American, Native American, Aleut, Asian Indian, Asian Pacific American, Eskimo, Hasidic Jew, Puerto Rican, and Spanish-speaking Americans." (Commerce.gov.)

- The Treasury Department has a grant to "authorize the Internal Revenue Service to enter into agreements with private or public nonprofit agencies or organizations to establish a network of trained volunteers to provide free income tax information and return preparation assistance to elderly taxpayers." (Treasury.gov.)

So as you can see, yes there are grants available, but maybe a better description would be "contracts." Free money for a business—no. Federal contract/grant to further a project—yes.

The best place to go to learn more about government contracts is a program called Business Matchmaking. Part of the Small Business Administration and very ably administered by SMA Global, this great program matches corporate and government procurement buyers with small business owners and sellers. If you are looking to get a government or corporate contract, then this is *the* program to check out (www.BusinessMatchmaking.com).

One of the problems most often encountered by businesses when they want to apply for a federal grant is actually finding out where to apply. To remedy that situation, the government put together the Grants.gov Web portal. It is designed to be the "central storehouse" for information relating to over 1,000 grant programs totaling more than $500 billion in funds. Note: Most of these awards go to state and local governments, universities, and nonprofits. Only a very small percentage goes to private industry.

Aside from Grants.gov, another good place to search for federal grants and contracts is the portal for the Catalogue of Federal Domestic Assistance—www.cfda.gov. I also recommend the search tool at Federal-Grants.com—www.federalgrants.com/search.php.

Additionally, you might consider conducting an online search for the terms "business grants" and the name of the federal agency that may need your goods or services. These departments include:

- Department of Agriculture
- Department of Commerce
- Department of Defense
- Department of Education
- Department of Energy
- Department of Health and Human Services
- Department of Homeland Security
- Department of Housing and Urban Development
- Department of the Interior
- Department of Justice
- Department of Labor
- Department of State
- Department of Transportation
- Department of the Treasury
- Department of Veterans Affairs

Again, it is best to think of these sorts of opportunities as federal contracts rather than grants. If you do that, then the answer is that yes there are literally billions of dollars available for small businesses in the way of government contracts.

Training grants. There is also some grant money available to help companies train employees to develop work skills. Start with the US Department of Labor's Business Relations Group website—www.doleta.gov/business.

In addition, state economic-development agencies also offer some training assistance, grants, and tax credits. For example, "The Illinois Employer Training Investment Program (ETIP) supports Illinois workers' efforts to upgrade their skills in order to remain current in new technologies and business practices, enabling companies to remain competitive, expand into new markets and introduce more efficient technologies into their operations. ETIP grants may reimburse Illinois companies for up to 50 percent of the cost of training their employees." (www.commerce.state.il.us.)

In addition, your local community college or public university may offer subsidized training programs and can help you with grant applications.

Technology grants. When it comes to getting one of these big-time, real grants, maybe the best place to tap into the federal R&D money pipeline is the government's Small Business Innovation Research (SBIR) and its Small Business Technology Transfer (STTR) programs. The SBIR/STTR does in fact offer grants to technology companies that undertake scientific R&D projects that have a high likelihood of having commercial applications. When you are looking for a federal grant, this is your best bet.

> "BIRMINGHAM, Ala. (BUSINESS WIRE) Agenta Biotechnologies, Inc., a private biotechnology company, announced that it has received a $1.1 million grant from the National Institutes of Health and National Institute of Dental and Craniofacial Research (NIH/NIDCR) for the further development of a biologically activated membrane to improve soft tissue healing associated with oral surgery. This grant is funded by the Small Business Innovative Research (SBIR) program."

The SBIR/STTR grants are offered by the following federal agencies and departments:

- Department of Agriculture
- Department of Commerce
- National Institute of Standards and Technology (NIST)
- National Oceanic and Atmospheric Agency (NOAA)
- Department of Defense
- Department of Education
- Department of Energy
- Department of Health and Human Services
- National Cancer Institute
- Department of Homeland Security
- Department of Transportation
- Environmental Protection Agency
- NASA
- National Science Foundation
- US Small Business Administration

For more information, go to SBIR.gov.

STATE GRANTS

You will have a better chance of receiving a government grant from your state than from the federal government, but even so, all of the aforementioned caveats apply here as well. Grants are not given to entrepreneurs to start new businesses. There is no free lunch. Grants *are* given to entrepreneurs who can help their state promote economic activity or otherwise foster a valued social cause like creating jobs. You might be able to locate a state grant, for instance, to help expand child care, or to create green technologies, or to promote tourism.

Every state has some sort of economic development agency intended to spur the economy of that state (although the agency may be called by a different name). That agency will list any grants that may be available. You can find the appropriate agency for your state by going to www.ecodevdirectory.com.

APPLYING FOR A GRANT

Whether it be a state or federal grant, make no mistake about it, finding and applying for the right grant will take time and tenacity. The requirements are stringent and the task is arduous. As the website Federal-Grants.com says, "The hardest time you will ever have applying for a federal grant is the first time. However, it does get easier with each federal grant you apply for and each of your grant applications will be better than the one previous."

The actual process of applying for a grant looks like this:

1. *Self-analysis.* FederalGrants.com says it best: "Applying for federal grants is one thing; being a federal grantee is another." Are you ready? Can you handle the increased workload the grant would entail? Are you prepared to be monitored by, and report to, the agency administering the grant?
2. *Find the right grants.* The sites previously mentioned will help you find the grants available to your business.
3. *Understand the requirements.* You need to understand both the technical requirements of the grant itself, as well as the grant-writing

process. Read and re-read the application carefully. These applications are not easy to fill out; this is the government, after all.

4. *Write the grant proposal.* Fill out the form, draft your proposal, and add any additional documentation necessary. This could be 30 pages or more. Be complete and accurate.

5. *Offer value.* Explain in the grant proposal not only what you propose to do, but also how it will benefit the agency and its goals. Show your expertise, vision, and experience.

6. *Submit.* It may be a physical application or it may be a virtual one; either way, be sure to submit it on time. Tardiness is usually not excused.

GOVERNMENT LOANS AND FUNDS

Federal loans. On the federal level, you already know what the 800-pound gorilla is when it comes to loans—namely, SBA loans. But the good news is that that is not the only game in town. There are a wide variety of loan programs available for businesses from various federal agencies and departments. For instance:

> *The Department of Agriculture, Business & Industrial loans.* The purpose of the "Business & Industrial (B&I) Guaranteed Loan Program is to improve, develop, or finance business, industry, and employment and improve the economic and environmental climate in rural communities."

> *SBA, Small Business Investment Company (SBIC) loans.* These loans and this program offer equity capital and long-term loans to qualifying small businesses.

> *Bureau of Indian Affairs, the Indian Loan Guaranty, Insurance, and Interest Subsidy Program.* This program assists businesses in obtaining financing from private sources to aid the economies of Indian reservations.

Of course, there are many, many more, in all sorts of areas and promoting all sorts of policies. Some are geared specifically toward minorities. Others are for women or veterans. To learn about all of these various programs you can thankfully go to one of the following two spots:

- The government's online loan portal, GovLoans.gov
- The government's business portal, Business.gov/financing

> "Business.gov is the US Government's official website for small businesses. Business.gov is the only government service to provide access to federal, state and local government from a single website. Small business owners no longer need to visit multiple websites to find forms, contact info, guidance with laws and regulations, and help applying for government assistance programs."

In addition to federal agency loan programs, if you are involved in the import or export of goods, you should also know about the Export-Import Bank of the United States, also called the Ex-Im Bank. The Ex-Im Bank provides financing assistance to US companies engaged in the exporting of goods to international markets. By offering the financing that many private institutions will not, the Ex-Im Bank assumes a greater portion of the risk. Think of it like an SBA loan for exporting—Ex-Im loans are made by private financial institutions, but are guaranteed up to 90 percent by the Ex-Im Bank. Funds can be used as working capital to run your business. For more information, go to Exim.gov.

State resources. While there are obviously some excellent federal resources, there is equal (if not more) action on the state and local level. Why? Especially in these economic times, state and local governments are aggressively trying to lure businesses to their area. Therefore, they have created a variety of incentive, economic, and loan programs and funds intended to do just that. This is a huge boon to entrepreneurs seeking funding. By locating the different programs in your area you may find a plethora of resources to help you get ahead.

Examples:

- Asphalt Recovery Technology is a company that recycles used asphalt roofing and turns it into various other products. The owners needed a significant infusion of money for equipment updates and labor costs but their bank loan was denied. Undaunted, they applied for a $1 million loan from a local economic development, government-funded nonprofit that administered a fund to lend money to companies that could foster job creation in the area. The company ended up receiving $800,000 at 7.75 percent and in return was required to create 25 jobs within three years.

- Portland, Oregon, wanted to become more business-friendly and attract more startups, so it created the Portland Seed Fund. Begun with a $500,000 infusion from the general fund, the city created a new entity called Bridge City Ventures. The fund then sought additional funding from other agencies and angel investors, all with the hope of providing early-stage startup financing. It expects to grow the fund to over $2 million.
- A policy of the state of California is to assist entrepreneurs start and grow businesses that have the potential to help the California economy. Therefore, the state created a program akin to the federal SBA loan guarantee system. The California Small Business Loan Guarantee program helps businesses get loans they otherwise could not qualify for and also helps those businesses establish a positive credit rating. The program guarantees up to 90 percent of a loan, for up to seven years, not to exceed $500,000.

There are many of these types of programs in all different locations and geared toward all sorts of different industries, so it would behoove you to find the ones in your area. That said, the bad news is that locating these sorts of programs is not always easy. There really is no one-stop shop as there is on the federal level, so it is a matter of digging in and drilling down. Online, check with the business sections of the websites of your city, county, and state. Aside from online research, another option is to visit your local Small Business Development Center (SBDC). The SBDCs are part of the SBA and are usually affiliated with universities. The SBDC in your area should likely be a storehouse of local government funding options.

COMMUNITY DEVELOPMENT FINANCIAL INSTITUTIONS

On the local level, you should also check out Community Development Financial Institutions (CDFIs). These are community institutions that serve struggling communities and underserved populations. While CDFIs do a lot more than provide affordable loans to needy small businesses (such as mortgages for homebuyers, financing for rental housing rehabilitation, and other needed financial services required by low-income households), a main focus is in fact serving less affluent small business communities with financial services and funding.

The CDFI business-development loans originate from funds made available by the Department of Housing and Urban Development, the Economic Development Administration, the Department of Agriculture, and other federal sources. The different local CDFI programs and institutions vary by name, but there are more than 1,000 of them nationwide, including:

- Community development banks
- Community development credit unions
- Community development loan funds
- Community development venture capital funds
- Microenterprise development loan funds
- Community development corporations

The preceding list provides the phrases you should Google.

According to CDFI.org: "While the term 'community development financial institutions' or 'CDFI' is relatively new, the concept itself is part of a rich history of self-help credit. From the immigrant guilds of New York City's Lower East Side and the Prairie Populists of the late 1800s, to African-American communities forming the first community development credit unions in the 1930s, communities have sought self-help credit solutions because traditional financial institutions have ignored or abandoned them."

Bottom Line: Governments at all levels want to help your business succeed because it is good for their respective economies. Research and take advantage of the many great programs that are out there.

CHAPTER 13

Partnerships

Essential Idea: Find a Partner Who Has the Money You Do Not

Marty and Phil met soon after college while both were working at a furniture store. Phil sold carpet and Marty handled advertising. They hit it off famously and before long started talking about going into business together. Marty had always dreamed of being an entrepreneur and Phil learned that he did not like working for someone else. Before long, they scraped together a little money, rented a 900-square-foot space, and opened their own carpet store, their dream.

They were a great team. Phil knew carpet, and Dad, I mean Marty, knew marketing, and before long, that one store multiplied, becoming two, then four, and then eight. At that point, they opened a beautiful, big new store that they made their headquarters. Marty and Phil shared one large office because, well, they were partners and liked working together.

As the years went by, they grew the chain to 17 stores. They made a good living, but also found that, after many years together, they did not see eye to eye that much any longer. Marty had become more manager than entrepreneur and did not like that. Phil had his own gripes. They grew weary of one another.

After many great years together, the partners decided that one of them had to go. After much bickering, my dad eventually sold his share of the business to Phil and used the proceeds to open a single, giant carpet warehouse where he was the only boss and entrepreneur. He loved that. Phil went on to run the chain and he loved that.

So yes, partnerships can be great, and they can also be terrible, but either way, they are definitely a popular way to go insofar as obtaining funding is concerned. There essentially are two sorts of partners— active, hands-on, participatory partners (called "general partners"), and passive, hands-off, at-a-distance partners (either a silent or limited partnership). The type you want and may get will depend on your goals and needs, and equally, the desires and expectations of the potential partner. If you want a silent partner but he or she wants to be an active partner, what you have instead is a problem. So step one really is determining which type of partner you want.

What type is best for you? Let's see.

GENERAL PARTNERSHIPS GENERALLY

Before drilling down into the money aspect of finding a partner, it is important to first understand the other characteristics of having a partner because they are not insignificant. A general partnership is the union of two or more people to carry on a business for profit. Partners have equal say in the business, and importantly, equal liabilities for it as well. Decisions should be made jointly, but legally can be made individually. Trust is required to make a general partnership work effectively. In fact, when a partnership works, the results can be great, as in the case, mostly, of Marty and Phil. But when they do not work out, partnerships can be disastrous. Unfortunately, my dad and Phil never spoke again after their partnership ended.

So yes, there are pros and cons. It is a choice that needs to be analyzed carefully. Does having someone who has the money outweigh having that person tell you what to do? Only you can decide. The first thing to appreciate is that, like the business marriage it is, a partnership is both a legal and an emotional commitment. You have to be in agreement and compatible on both levels.

Here are four tips to making any partnership work:

1. *Test before you buy.* A general partnership is, first and foremost, a legal arrangement. For instance, did you know that your partner could take on debt in the partnership's name and not tell you about it, and

yet you would still be liable for it? That's true. As I said, it is legally a lot like a marriage.

So before jumping in, it is a good idea to test the waters first. Live together for a while, as it were. Do a project together. Do your styles mesh? Do you clash? You want to discover whether you work well together, if you agree more than you disagree, and if it is fun, because if it is not, then no matter how much money the person is willing to invest in your business, it won't be worth it.

> **What to look for in a partner: You want someone whom you can trust and whose values match yours. You want someone who is honest. Importantly and ideally, this should be someone whose skills complement and augment your own. Finally, you want someone you can spend 10 hours a day with and enjoy their company.**

2. *Even it out.* The good news about a general partnership is that you will in fact have someone with whom to work, someone to kibbitz with, and (ideally) someone who has money to put in the business. But to be really effective, make sure you divide the workload evenly, and according to your strengths. Resentment builds when one partner (and often, it is the one who put in more money) seemingly has too much power or control. Beware of that.

3. *Be reasonable.* Especially if you are used to running a business on your own, having a partner can cramp your style. You will now need to share responsibilities and, more importantly, decisions. To avoid troubles, agree to give each other a wide berth; you do your job and they do theirs. And don't make the mistake of Marty and Phil—avoid working in too close proximity with one another, if possible.

4. *Have a vision.* The best partnerships, in business and in life, happen when the partners have a joint vision for where they want to go. Make sure you and your partner will be on the same page.

So the good news is that you will have a partner. The bad news is, you will have a partner.

Partners with money. Of course, you don't want just any partner; you are looking for a partner with money. Remember that what you will be offering is qualitatively different than what a partner with money will offer, and as such your job is doubly difficult. Not only must you take into account all of the caveats and responsibilities just listed, but moreover, you must figure out how to make what easily can be an unequal relationship equal. I say it will be inherently unequal at the start because money is power. Even if the new partner knows he is buying into a great business, it remains true that, if he also knows you need the money, then he is in a position of power and leverage. That is human nature.

What you have to offer is different. It is your sweat equity, meaning your hard work, commitment, vision, passion, and either a business or business plan. Sweat equity is your human contribution to, and efforts in, the business. While sweat equity sometimes seems not as valuable as real capital, it is not unimportant. Think of it in terms of a real estate deal. Your partner may put in the $10,000 necessary for the down payment, but if you are the one who is able to redo the bathroom and add a deck onto the house, your contribution is no less important.

Your challenge will be to find a partner who appreciates the sweat equity you can bring to the party. What you do not want is a partner who thinks that his money is more important than your efforts, one who thinks he is superior. That is a partner whose money will never be worth his bad attitude.

Where to find monied partners. The best place to begin is with the usual suspects. Put the word out to your network of friends and family members. Given that they know you best and know your plan or business, they can be excellent business matchmakers. In addition, speak with your accountant, lawyer, banker, and real estate agent, and with people where you worship. Let them know you need a business partner interested in investing in the business.

Another rich vein to mine are people in your industry. Speak with colleagues, sales reps, and if you have a business already, possibly even employees and customers (though caution is advised there). Again, because these are people who know you and the business, they may be a great resource for matching you with the people they know who may be interested in the sort of opportunity you can present.

> If you already own a business and are looking for a partner, it is vital that you get a current business valuation first. Without knowing what your business is really worth, you cannot adequately analyze how a potential partner's contribution should be valued. If your business is worth $100,000, a $25,000 investment means a lot more than if the business is worth $250,000.

Beyond traditional networking, here are several more ways to seek and find a potential business partner with cash to invest:

- Advertise. The "Business Opportunities" classified section in the Sunday paper, in trade magazines, and on websites can be a potential goldmine. Who reads these sections? People interested in some sort of business opportunity, that's who! If you have one, advertise there for a partner.
- As with the quest for an angel investor, the search for a business partner can be aided by social media. By having a strong presence on LinkedIn, Twitter, and Facebook, you can very effectively put the word out about your desire for a partner, your requirements, and your needs.
- Check out the website BusinessPartners.com. This is an online database of investors looking to partner up with the right business.
- The angel investor directories listed in that previous chapter may also be a good source for locating an equity partner, though usually they will look to be silent partners and not active general partners.

As with any online resource, of course, the research part is just the start. When you are looking for someone to invest in your business, either actively or passively, you must get to know that person well—up close and personal, as the saying goes. You will need to check out their story, references, and credit history.

SILENT PARTNERS

A silent partner is a passive investor in the business. A silent partner is not involved in the day-to-day operations of a business and typically is only concerned with its profitability. They have equal rights to profits, as well as equal rights to liabilities and debts, and of course that can be an issue. If there is a lawsuit, for instance, silent partners can be brought into the fray just as much as you can, whether they are silent or not. That can scare off a lot of potential silent partners. If that is the case, the solution is to consider a limited partnership, as discussed next.

But the good news about silent partners (aside from their money, of course) is that, as opposed to an angel investor, they need not have any special knowledge or expertise in your line of business. It may be that they just like you, or the opportunity, and want a piece of the action. Way to go.

LIMITED PARTNERSHIPS

The final type of partnership that you can enter into, especially insofar as money goes, is a limited partnership. This is a very specific legal entity that has traditionally been used for real estate investments and motion picture financing.

With a general partnership, the partners all have equal say and equal liability. With a limited partnership, there is one general partner in charge of operations and one or several limited partners. Limited partners are like silent partners in that they have no say in the daily operations of the business, but they differ in that their exposure, their liability, is limited to the extent of their investment. That is a distinct advantage and benefit. They cannot be held liable for more than that amount. It helps to think of a limited partner as akin to a shareholder in a corporation—they have no real say but do get to share in any profits.

For your potential partner with cash, a limited partnership may be a very attractive option as it allows them to share in the profits without incurring more risk and liability than necessary.

PARTNERSHIPS AGREEMENTS

Because there are so many moving parts to a partnership, it is vital that you put your agreement in writing. Think of a partnership agreement as a prenup for your business. It covers the worst-case scenario and dictates what will happen should the worst indeed come to fruition, because sometimes it does. Because of its importance, you need the assistance of a lawyer; you don't perform surgery on yourself, and likewise, you should not represent yourself in legal matters as important as a partnership agreement.

Your partnership agreement should cover at least the following:

- Identification as to what sort of partnership is being created.
- Identification of who invested how much, how partnership shares are to be divided, and how profits are to be distributed.
- The rights, responsibilities, and duties of each partner.
- If and how partnership shares can be transferred.
- Exit strategies.
- How to oust a partner.
- Causes of dissolution, and distribution of assets upon dissolution.
- Salaries.

Bottom Line: Finding a partner with money to invest in you and your business may not be easy, but it can be done, and can prove to be a great asset to your business in many ways beyond the financial. Choose the sort of partnership that bests fits your respective interests.

CHAPTER 14

Mergers and Strategic Alliances

Essential Idea: Find Another Business Willing to Invest in Your Business

As the eighteenth-century Scottish poet Robert Burns once noted, the best laid plans of mice and men often go awry. That certainly was the case with one of the most famous, and definitely the largest, merger of all time: that of AOL and Time Warner in the year 2000, valued at a whopping $350 billion.

The master plan was to merge the old world media of Time Inc. with the new e-world dominance of America Online. The result was supposed to be a business behemoth that would annihilate everything in its way. When the deal was announced, Steve Case, a cofounder of AOL, called it a "historic moment in which new media has truly come of age." Gerald Levin, the CEO of Time Warner, saw the merger in even bigger terms. At the time, Levin said, "The values that we feel we can leave as a legacy . . . have a lot to do with the social destiny of people everywhere." (*Time* magazine, January 24, 2000.)

The best laid plans . . .

The new conglomerate never meshed, let alone found synergy from the combination of old and new media. The company proved to be too big, too clunky, too disparate. The AOL–Time Warner stock price tumbled, there were investigations by the SEC and Justice Department, and in the end, the combined value of the companies once they split again, late in the decade, was about one-seventh of their value on the day of the merger.

Ted Turner was the largest shareholder in the combined company and he eventually lost 80 percent of his wealth because of the deal, some $8 billion total. Says Turner, "The Time Warner–AOL merger should pass into history like the Vietnam War. . . . [It's] one of the biggest disasters that have occurred to our country." (*New York Times*, January 10, 2010.) Today, according to that *New York Times* article, business schools teach that the transaction was "the worst in history."

Beyond the financial ramifications of the fiasco, of relevance here are the unintended consequences that can result from a merger or strategic partnership. Maybe Steve Case said it best in the *Times*: "The day of the announcement was bittersweet, frankly. On the one hand, obviously, it was an exciting time in bringing together the leading Internet company and the leading media company to create a new company that really had the potential to lead in this new century. At the same time, I recognized that my role was going to change." Boy, did it ever.

So the challenge and opportunity when considering mergers and strategic alliances is to take the new without losing the best of the old.

MERGERS AND ACQUISITIONS (M&A)

There are all sorts of reasons two businesses may want to become one, but in the context of business funding, the case almost always is one where one company has far less available capital than another and needs the money from the other. In that case, the company in need of cash seeks to merge or be acquired by another company in order to get a capital infusion of some sort. It is not unlike a partnership between entrepreneurs where one has the cash and the other offers sweat equity, only in this case it is the combining of two businesses instead of two people.

There are various ways a company can merge with another, including:

- One company acquires all of the assets and liabilities of another company. This is the most common method. In this case, the company being acquired gets cash but thereafter typically ceases to exist.
- One company buys all of another company's assets.
- One company buys all of another company's stock.

Whatever the case, the main reason is usually economic; the two businesses think that the combined company will be more valuable together than if they remained separate. This may occur, for example, where one company has access to a different customer base, or there may be economies of scale that can occur by joining forces, or there are products and services one company offers that the other does not.

Whatever the case, if you are seeking funding for your business and are considering the M&A route, there are two important factors to keep in mind.

The first is that you have to offer another company something they do not already have; they have no reason to invest in your business otherwise. The second is that, in the typical merger, the "needier" company gets bought out. As such, unless you want to go out of business, a merger may not be the solution to your money issues. And since the point of this book is to help you find the money you need to run your business rather than finding the money you need by going out of business, the 100 percent merger option will not be discussed further.

The other way to go is to do a partial merger; that is, you sell part of your company or assets to another business in order to get a cash infusion. Think of when IBM sold its ThinkPad division to Lenovo—that is a partial acquisition. It infused IBM with a significant sum of money and turned Lenovo into, well, Lenovo.

> One reason the IBM sale of its ThinkPad division to Lenovo succeeded as well as it did was that IBM retained about a 14 percent share in ThinkPad, even after the sale. In addition, Lenovo was able to convince IBM to contribute some of its top executives to the new Lenovo ThinkPad division. As a result, IBM had a stake in Lenovo succeeding.

In the case of a partial acquisition, success in the selling of an asset, of getting the funding you need and still remaining successful, is threefold.

First, you must have an asset that is worth buying and that you can part with without it too severely affecting the rest of your business. If, for instance, you have a piece of raw land that you can afford to part with, then the sale should be simple and straightforward. Conversely, if you have a product line that is vital to your bottom line, portioning it off and selling it would likely be quite problematic. So your first challenge is to figure out what it is that you can afford to sell.

Second, you have to correctly value that asset—not only to your potential buyer, but to your business as well. The sale of that empty lot is a good example. Let's assume it sits next door to Freddie's Furniture Factory and Freddie wants it for additional parking. This is not the same as a fair market valuation since to you it is an empty lot, but to Freddie it is a solution. It is more valuable to him than to you. A fair market valuation of the lot may not tell the whole story. In any case, you need to be able to value the asset.

Valuing a profit center, on the other hand, is not easy, but it can be done. One common method is called the multiplier. What you do here is to take your net profit of that division and multiply it by some number, typically between two and four, which corresponds to a number of years. It works this way: A profit center that nets you $50,000 a year with a two-year multiplier means that it is worth $100,000 over the next two years to the buyer. The negotiation, as you may surmise, is over what the proper multiplier is. You want it bigger; they want it smaller.

The final consideration has to do with finding the right company with which to do business. There likely will be strategic considerations at play, such as:

- Do you want to sell this asset to a competitor?
- What will it do to your business if this new business gains your asset?
- How will you be able to use the capital you receive to grow your business?
- Will you need to help the new business with the transition, and if so, are you willing to do that?
- If it is not an outright sale, how well do you mesh with the acquiring company?

That last point is critical. There are plenty of M&As, especially where we are talking about a partial acquisition, where the two companies do not really fit well together, as was the case of AOL and Time Warner. And it also was the case in that merger that one of the critical factors leading to its failure was a clash of cultures. The two companies did not mix. That is what you must consider carefully. You will need to locate a partner with whom you can work, whose values and vibe you share.

Reasons one company may want to buy another company's asset: (1) to make more money, (2) to reduce costs, (3) for tax benefits, (4) for operational efficiencies, (5) to better compete in the overall marketplace, (6) to better compete against a particular competitor, (7) to increase market share, (8) for better distribution, and (9) for vanity and branding.

Finding a company willing to buy your assets may actually not be as difficult as it sounds. Although this is not a case where putting out the word to your personal network will help (since a friend of your uncle's probably has no interest in purchasing your product line), putting out the word to your business network *can* help. Your business colleagues and yes, even your competitors are prime candidates, so your job is to let them know what you have for sale and your interest in finding the right partner.

Using your competition to get your business funded—what a diabolically clever idea!

STRATEGIC ALLIANCES

Mergers and strategic alliances are similar in that both involve two businesses teaming up in one way or another. But that is where the similarities end. It is their differences that are far more striking. Whereas a merger (all or part) involves the *sale* of a prime business asset to another firm, a strategic alliance is the *sharing* of mutually beneficial assets and therefore requires that the two businesses meet as equals to accomplish a goal.

Because you are the party seeking the funding, you must bring something to the joint venture that the other business wants, something they do not have that is of value to them. Contacts, contracts, partners, distribution channels, customers, marketing know-how, property, venues, copyrights, patents, trade secrets—it could be almost anything. Whatever it is, if you are going to trade its value in for some cash, it must be something the other company needs.

Here are the different sorts of relationships that you should explore when seeking a strategic partnership as a fund-raising tool:

Teaming with a larger company. They have the money and you have the something else. The trick will be to get them to value your asset fairly. Again, you simply must have something unique to offer that they cannot attain without your assistance.

Teaming with an existing customer. Teaming up and doing some sort of deal or alliance with one of your existing customers makes a lot of sense and has a high likelihood of success. After all, they already know you and your business, and like it. They buy from you, after all. They know what you do and you know what to expect. Finding a way to further bolster your bond through a joint project is smart because it should not really look like you are seeking funding; rather, that you are seeking a better relationship. The bonus is that, aside from funding, you may also actually further cement that key relationship.

Teaming with a potential client. Maybe you have a former employer who might be interested in working with you. Maybe there is a brand leader who has funds available and is looking to tap a customer base like the one you have. The thing is, there are people out there who need what you have to offer. You job is to put out the feelers, find out who they are, and reel them in.

Teaming with the competition. This is more challenging because, whereas with a merger the competition ends when your asset or business is sold, with a strategic partnership you are seeking to help the competition. That is a tougher sell. One scenario that does work here is where you and the competition team up in order to compete even more effectively against an even larger competitor.

The enemy of my enemy is my friend.

"Shares of Adobe Systems soared yesterday on speculation the company may see a bid from Microsoft Corporation, which was fueled by a visit from Microsoft CEO Steve Ballmer to Adobe's headquarters. Apparently, Ballmer met with Adobe CEO Shantanu Narayen to discuss Apple's control over the smartphone market and how the two companies can collaborate to beat the maker of iPhone."

Source: BeaconEquity.com.

Bottom Line: While you probably do not want to be completely bought out in a merger, you can find the money you seek by either selling a strategic asset to a competitor in a partial merger or offering it to them for their use via a strategic partnership. Either scenario can net you some valuable capital.

SECTION

IV

Creative Online Options

CHAPTER 15

Peer-to-Peer Lending

Essential Idea: Go Online and Get Funding from Your Peers

Jennifer started her natural soap company in 2005 out of her home on a shoestring budget, a wing, and a few prayers. Within two years she was able to get her soaps into a few stores and created a nice online e-business profit center as well. The next year she was able to move her business into an office and adjacent warehouse. Things were looking up.

In 2008, a client asked her to create a shampoo line that it wanted to carry in their stores and privately brand. Thrilled, Jennifer immediately applied for a loan at a bank. But since this was right around the time that the economic tsunami hit, she was turned down. She tried again at her personal credit union, still to no avail. She lacked both the requisite great credit rating and necessary valuable collateral.

Jennifer did not know what to do but was afraid of missing out on the incredible business opportunity that was in front of her. Then she heard about a relatively recent phenomenon called peer-to-peer (P2P) lending, which is sort of like social networking for money. Businesses seeking funding can post their business opportunities online and then investors can peruse the offerings, find the loans they like, bid on them, and if they win, fund them.

Using online P2P lending, Jennifer was able to craft a pitch about the opportunity and post it on one of the P2P sites that have recently sprung up online. Within a few weeks she secured the $20,000 she needed to create, bottle, and ship her new product.

Online peer-to-peer lending is a seemingly clever idea whose time may have come, but not without problems. Indeed, it sounds almost too good to be true: Bypass banks altogether, cut out the mean middleman, offer affordable repayment terms, and locate investors who have the foresight and ability to personally fund projects and businesses large and small. Is it right for you? If your money needs are not great (most loans cap out at $25,000), if you have an opportunity that intrigues people, and if you are a good credit risk, it just may be. But know this too: it is not for everybody and the chances of getting funded this way are not necessarily high.

HOW P2P LENDING WORKS

Let's start with the bad news: Although peer-to-peer lending made a big splash when it first hit the market in 2007 or so, there were many ensuing bumps along the road. The major ones were that investors lost a lot of money investing in the small businesses that initially populated these P2P sites; businesses that looked better on paper than they were in reality.

Since then, the good news is that things are tighter and more uniform now. Those problems are receding. But that also means that fewer projects are getting accepted to these sites for possible funding and fewer still are getting funded.

That said, there are still businesses that do get accepted and funded. Step one is to find the right site for your business. There are several P2P sites from which to choose. The main ones are:

- Prosper.com
- LendingClub.com

Once you choose a site or sites, the next step in the P2P process is to fill out the online loan request form and profile. Being able to post your request on these various sites is not automatic. Like any good lender, the P2P sites now have stringent credit standards. At Lending Club, your debt-to-income ratio must be below 25 percent and you must have a FICO score of at least 660. At Prosper, it's 640. If you do not meet these standards you will not be able to post your request on the site. Once that happens, P2P sites offer instantaneous feedback, so you will know immediately if you qualify to post your project on the site (and it is free to fill out the request form to see if you do in fact qualify).

Assuming you do qualify, you also will immediately see what sort of interest rate you qualify for. At the time of this writing, interest rates ranged from a low of around 6 percent to a high near 20 percent. As with anything in the world of credit and money, the better your credit score, the lower the interest rate and the better the repayment terms you will get.

Once you pass this first hurdle, you then need to craft your pitch. Your loan request profile will describe you, your business, how much you want to borrow, and why. The site will post your credit information and FICO score along with your loan request and profile.

Once your project and request are posted, lenders then have the chance to review them in the context of all of the other loan requests on the site. The different sites each run things a little differently at this stage. At Prosper.com, for example, investors bid on the loans, naming the amount they would like to lend and at what interest rate. A borrower with a good credit rating and equally good plan could expect to get several offers and then choose the one with the best terms and lowest interest rate. Riskier loans may get no bids at all.

> One of the main things to understand if you want to get your P2P loan request funded is that P2P lenders are people lending to people; they gravitate to these sorts of sites because they like the human aspect of the investment. Accordingly, you increase your chances of getting funded if, aside from having a good credit score and sound business plan, you also have a good story. Let people know who you are. Be honest and transparent. Post pictures of yourself and your business. People like to invest in people more than businesses.

Most of these sites have a time limit for each posting. At Lending Club it is two weeks. If you do not have a full funding offer within that time frame, you will have to either accept any partial funding offers that you have received or repost the request for another two-week period.

Once the deal is set to be consummated, the actual process is that the investor does not personally loan the money to the entrepreneur; rather, it loans it to the P2P site, which issues a promissory note that the borrower will pay on. The site takes a small fee for processing the incoming money, making the note, and funding the actual loan. Therefore, while such sites like to boast that they "eliminate the middleman," the truth is somewhat more muddled. That middleman has simply been replaced by another: the P2P middleman.

FEES AND COSTS

The amount you will pay for the loan you get depends on several factors:

- Your credit score.
- The overall economic environment.
- The length of the loan (P2P loans typically do not last more than three years).

In addition to the interest you will pay, there are also—no surprise here—closing costs, between 0.5 percent and 5 percent.

Example: You get a $5,000 loan for three years and have decent but not great credit. You would be assessed a $150 closing fee, and thus would receive upon closing $4,850. At a 15.5 percent interest rate, you would be repaying the loan at about $170 a month.

PROS AND CONS

The *Harvard Business Review* (February 6, 2009) called peer-to-peer lending "one of the breakout ideas of 2009" but again, that was before some of the problems that soon became apparent in this new industry were in fact seen.

On the surface, P2P lending has many things going for it. It offers cash-strapped entrepreneurs a whole new platform for seeking potential investors. It is quick and easy. The benefits to the lender are no less potentially appealing: P2P lending offers competitive rates of return, there are many businesses from which to choose, and lenders can see a tangible result as a consequence of their investment. All in all, these are good.

> According to the website Peer-Lend, P2P borrowers "can receive better interest rates, and investors can yield better returns on invested funds." These P2P sites typically claim that their investment notes offer annualized returns of around 9 or 10 percent. But such returns don't come without risk. The Prosper.com prospectus says, "The Notes (loans) are highly risky and speculative" and "Investing . . . should be considered only by persons who can afford the loss of their entire investment."

But there are definite and major downsides to this sort of lending that may not be apparent at first blush.

Regulatory and legal issues. Loans and investments are subject to governmental regulation, and properly satisfying such regulations and regulators is not easy. Maybe that is why one of these sites had to shut down for a while, as it sought SEC compliance. That is very troubling.

Availability. P2P lending sites, while seemingly national, in fact are not able to operate in many states. Check the maps of the sites to see if they are available in your state.

Overly emotional. One of the assets of this sort of personal banking is equally detrimental. Investment decisions should be made on the qualifications of the business, nothing else.

Repayment. For the lender, because the investment is unsecured, there is no guarantee of a return. Lending unsecured money to people you do not know may not be a sound investment strategy. Lenders have lost money—a lot of money.

WHERE TO GO FROM HERE?

Online peer-to-peer lending is a relatively new and recent phenomenon. As with almost any new industry, there were bound to be kinks and rough spots that needed to be smoothed over. So, while this funding option offers a lot of promise, it is not without risk to both the borrower and the lender. Be smart and do your homework.

Bottom Line: P2P loans are not easy to get, and the interest rate can be astronomical, so be careful. Indeed, P2P lending issues illustrate why banks are still professional and excellent lending options. Carefully check out the P2P site you choose.

CHAPTER **16**

Crowdfunding

Essential Idea: Get People to Invest in Your Cause in Exchange for Something Other Than Money

Crowdfunding has been around for a while, but the term is very new. One of its first incarnations was back in the 1992 presidential election, which Bill Clinton eventually won. But before he garnered the nomination, he was in a heated primary battle with a slew of better-known Democrats, ex-California Governor Jerry Brown among them.

As the primary season moved on, and as Clinton slowly emerged as the front-runner, the other candidates began to withdraw one by one as their money and votes dried up: Paul Tsongas, Tom Harkin, Bob Kerry. But Brown was able to stick around and grind it out against the popular Arkansas governor because he hit upon a then-unique strategy: Brown created an 800 number and asked people to call in and donate to his campaign. He would accept donations of no more than $100. In these pre-Internet days, this was a revolutionary way to tap a lot of money by asking for a little amount of money from a lot of people.

Jerry Brown crowdfunded his campaign.

More recently, filmmaker Kieran Masterton was able to successfully crowdfund his startup—a film distribution business called OpenIndie .com. Masterton says that his month-long crowdfunding campaign netted his business more than $12,000 in funding, along with some great publicity and a "built-in audience and user base for our site." ("How to

Crowdfund Your Startup" by Kieran Masterton, ThinkVitamin.com, April 22, 2010.)

So, just what is crowdfunding (also sometimes called crowd financing or crowd-sourced capital)?

Let's see.

CROWDFUNDING IS DIFFERENT

Throughout this book we have looked at a variety of ways to get people to believe in you and invest in your business—everything from bank loans to partners to peer-to-peer lending. And in every one of those, the person making the investment and commitment of money expects to be paid back with money.

Not here. Crowdfunding is different. With crowdfunding, an individual has a business or project that needs a certain amount of capital to move forward. That aspect is the same. The entrepreneur looks for people willing to take a chance on this vision. That too is the same. But here's the kicker: Instead of getting repaid with cash, the crowdfunding investor accepts some other type of "reward" as payment, in lieu of money.

What sort of reward, you ask? Maybe not what you would expect. Typically, the rewards have something to do with the business or project. A filmmaker looking for financing for his movie might offer a credit at the end in exchange for an investment of, say, $100. A restaurant may name a sandwich after a larger investor in the business. The aforementioned Kieran Masterton tells the story of a woman who needed a new hull for her boat for her trip around the world and promised a postcard from her many stops along the way to investors, and even that worked.

As you can see, this is a creative process wherein the investors appreciate that being repaid with money or equity in the business is not the only way to be rewarded for taking a risk and financial patronage.

Take the case of Masterton's OpenIndie.com, for example. These entrepreneurs had a unique business model for a movie distribution business: Instead of a "push" method, wherein the distributor pushes movies out to different locations, OpenIndie is a "pull" method, whereby people go on the site and pull the movies they like to their neighborhood.

So what Masterton and his team offered was a chance for 100 filmmakers to get listed on their site in exchange for a crowdfunding payment of $100. One hundred dollars times 100 filmmakers equals $10,000.

"Politicians do it. Charities too. And now for-profit entrepreneurs are tapping the Internet to get small amounts of money from lots and lots of supporters. One part social networking and one part capital accumulation, crowdfunding websites seek to harness the enthusiasm—and pocket money—of virtual strangers, promising them a cut of the returns."

Source: *Time* magazine, "Crowdfunding," September 4, 2008.

Another example is SellaBand.com, which offers a crowdfunding platform for musicians looking to create a new music project: "A new album, tour, or the promotion of their music." The artists post their profiles and music on the site, and music lovers offer help at $10 a "share." The site calls it "fan funding." Once the band reaches their goal, fans are repaid with "free downloads and other goodies artists might offer like exclusive CDs, t-shirts, free lunches, etc. And artists might even let you get a cut of their revenues." The great thing here is that not only do musicians get the money they need, but they end up creating a crowd of people invested in their success and who would be willing to buy more of their music down the road.

With crowdfunding, investors usually are given different levels of patronage offers. They may get X for investing $10, Super X for investing $50, and Ultimate X for investing $100. Crowdfunding is unique in that it seeks to raise a lot of money a little bit at a time. Usually, crowdfunding entrepreneurs do not seek thousands of dollars from individual investors; this is more of a three-figure investment than a four-figure investment.

So the idea here is to list your business or project on one of the crowdfunding sites, promote it, and offer investors some unique reward in exchange for their patronage. It is a different and clever way to get funded without having to pay your investors back with your limited capital. Of course there has to be some valuable, tangible benefit in it for them; otherwise they would not invest in you. But that is also part of the fun and juice in this. By offering a creative return for their investment, you can build your business via a network of fans who love what you do.

CROWDFUNDING SITES

With such a cool and interesting way to fund a business or project, it is no surprise that crowdfunding has taken off. A slew of sites have emerged online to facilitate the teaming of dreamer and believers. Some sites are geared toward specific industries or particular creative endeavors (like music), while others are more broadly applicable to all sorts of projects.

Here are some of the top choices:

KickStarter.com. KickStarter is one of the better-known names in the crowdfunding game. KickStarter offers a number of different categories like food, art, and technology. While listing a project is free, KickStarter retains 5 percent of all money raised, as well as a small portion of all credit card processing fees.

One of the unique things about KickStarter is that projects must raise 100 percent of their goal, or they get nothing. For example, if you are looking to raise $10,000 for your new studio, you need to raise all $10,000 before the funds are transferred from KickStarter. This is actually a smart thing as it protects investors and gives them the confidence necessary to invest. What if you raised only $1,300 for your studio? That would not be very fair to those investors since it could actually turn out to be a waste of their money. So the 100 percent requirement allows them to safely "test-drive" a project and helps you because it protects them.

The TikTok and LunaTik are products that take a small iPod Nano and turn it into an amazing wristwatch. The designer offered the following rewards on KickStarter: "A pledge of $1 or more helps make this project a reality. For $25 or more you are pre-ordering and will receive the TikTok Multi-Touch Watch Kit which will sell for $34.95 at retail. For a $50 pledge you are pre-ordering and will receive the LunaTik Multitouch Watch Conversion Kit. The LunaTik is hot-stamped and [made] out of aerospace grade aluminum. $150 or more gets you a serialized, red-anodized LunaTik KickStarter Backer Edition signed via laser by the designer."

The initial goal was to raise $15,000. The product proved so wildly popular, however, that 13,512 people invested $941,718.

IndieGoGo. IndieGoGo is a great site and resource and definitely one of the leaders in the crowdfunding field that calls itself a "collaborative way to fund ideas." IndieGoGo does not require 100 percent funding to move forward, but if you do not raise the full amount, they charge you more: 9 percent as opposed to 4 percent if you get fully funded. This idea is otherwise the same:

1. Create, customize, and publish an online funding campaign.
2. Raise awareness of it by sharing it with others on the site and elsewhere.
3. Collect contributions.
4. Track contributions using the site's dashboard.

GrowVC.com. GrowVC is a site just for startups and is a bit different than the other sites mentioned here. GrowVC labels itself "the Virtual Silicon Valley. Bringing the first truly global, transparent, community-based approach to seed-funding. Grow VC can help startups secure initial funding of up to $1M for their businesses."

As such, the idea is to create a VC fund, as a traditional VC firm would. The difference is that although GrowVC manages the fund, investment decisions are made by members, by the crowd. The members decide how much of their investment will go to which startups.

PROS AND CONS

The benefits of crowdfunding should be self-evident:

- It offers a unique funding mechanism.
- Typically, you do not have to repay people with cash.
- It offers you immediate feedback on the viability of your idea; bad ideas don't get funded.
- It creates word-of-mouth advertising.
- It also creates a built-in customer base of people who liked your business enough to invest in it.

The downsides are:

- Depending on the site, you may gain traction, but not enough traction.
- People may steal your great idea once they see it posted online.

- Significantly, there may be legal issues to navigate. Soliciting investments from the public is something regulated by the Securities and Exchange Commission. Check with the site and your attorney regarding this possibility.

CROWDFUNDING TIPS

Because one of the unique benefits of crowdfunding is that it gets people interested and invested (literally) in your business at a potentially very early stage, those folks can become your cheerleaders and advocates. Use that. Tap into that potential. Help them help you.

   Other things that have helped entrepreneurs successfully crowdfund include:

- *Use video.* On whatever crowdfunding site you choose, be sure to post a video explaining who you are, what the opportunity is, and how it can benefit the investor. Entrepreneurs who post videos raise more money.
- *Be specific.* The best crowdfunding projects offer detailed descriptions of the project. They identify the entrepreneur, the business, how the funds will be used, and what the investor will get in return. Make sure people understand why your request is necessary for your success.
- *Choose good rewards.* Yes, people who invest this way want to help you, but they also want something out of it. If you can tie the benefit directly into something valuable the investor will receive, that is best. OpenIndie.com allows investors to put their films on the site. Investors in TikTok watches got a watch. Using crowdfunding to presell your product works very well.
- *Deliver.* Whatever you promise, deliver on that promise.
- *Listen.* You are trying to appeal to a crowd. Ask them what they want, and then give them what they want.
- *Promote your project.* Once you list your business or project on the crowdfunding site, let people know it is there. Use the site promotion tools as well as your own resources to get the word out. As one crowdfunder said, "You cannot expect to just create a project and hope people discover it. It is exactly like when your band plays a show. If you don't post fliers everywhere and tell all your friends, you won't expect

many people to show up. You have to work for it. Post your project on Facebook, give your project info on Twitter! E-mail your friends!" (TheWebPunk.com.)

- *Work it..* As Kieran Masterton said in his article, "It took four weeks of tweeting, blogging, answering questions, doing interviews and, quite honestly, pimping the hell out of our campaign page to secure our $10,000."
- *Use your niche.* Masterton asked 100 filmmakers for $100. You could ask 100 salespeople, or 50 photographers.

Bottom Line: Crowdfunding is an excellent, new, and unique way to get your business funded. By appealing to both the altruistic and investor sensibilities of the crowd, finding the money you need is very possible.

Other Creative Options

CHAPTER 17

Microfinance

Essential Idea: Tap into the Growing Global Popularity of Microloans to Get the Funding You Need

Ryan Fochler had a dream. An animal lover by nature and entrepreneur at heart, Fochler was stuck in a corporate computer job back in the early 2000s. His dream was to start his own animal-related business. And so he did. By using savings and a home-equity line of credit (this peculiar funding mechanism was widely available back at this time when people apparently had something called "equity" in their homes). Fochler ventured out on his own to start a simple yet profitable dog-walking business.

The business grew steadily and by late 2007, Fochler had decided to expand. He got a loan from his bank and began to convert an old 7,000–square-foot pharmacy into a full-fledged pet day care and retail outlet. This was in mid-2008. And then it hit—the financial earthquake, just as he was in mid-construction. Almost immediately the bank froze his credit line. What was Ryan Fochler going to do?

Tap into microfinance, that's what.

Microfinance is an idea that is usually thought of in conjunction with third-world economies. Groups like Kiva.org and the Grameen Bank of Bangladesh lend small sums of money—microloans—to needy, would-be entrepreneurs. A typical microloan might be for, say, $100 to buy two cows.

Microloans have not generally been considered an option when discussing entrepreneurship in a Western economic setting.

Until now.

These days, microfinance is adapting its practices to the Western world, and that is what Ryan Fochler and his pet care business used. Fochler applied for and received a microloan from a local microlender in his area, the Latino Economic Development Corporation (LEDC). Whereas microlenders in poorer countries do in fact make tiny micro-loans, here in the United States, a more typical microloan is like those made by LEDC: The average size of an LEDC loan is $10,000, at a 10 percent interest rate. An American microloan might be for as little as $500. The maximum of such loans is usually $35,000.

> "Are you a small business owner looking to start, expand or improve your busi-ness? If you are seeking working capital, equipment, or marketing support, con-sider an LEDC loan to help finance your business needs. As a certified Community Development Financial Institution, LEDC provides micro-loans be-tween $500 and $50,000 to start-ups and existing businesses that have diffi-culty obtaining credit from mainstream financial institutions."
>
> Source: The Latino Economic Development Corporation (www.ledcmetro.org).

For Fochler, the LEDC microloan was a lifeline. His problem had not been profitability; his business grew at an average of about 170 percent a year. He had 25 employees. He was adding new profit centers. But what he did not have was sufficient collateral. As such, all of the other positives he offered were outweighed by that one negative. But what LEDC was more interested in was making sure Fochler ran a good business and that the loan would be paid back in full and on time. He did and it was.

Fochler got his money, and a lot of dogs are happier because of it.

MICROLENDING IN THE UNITED STATES

There are few good things to be said about the Great Recession, but one is this: a whole slew of new and creative methods for funding a business have come out of it (necessity being the mother of invention and all). One of these new funding mechanisms is the adaptation of traditional microfinance and microlending to richer economies. The needs are there; they are just different, both qualitatively and quantitatively. It turns out that Western entrepreneurs need microloans too— just tack on a zero or two.

In 2006, the Grameen Bank and its founder Muhammad Yunus received the Nobel Peace Prize. Interesting Grameen facts:

- Fully 97 percent of its borrowers are women.
- The bank requires no collateral.
- The repayment rate is 97.25 percent.
- Because it wants no litigation in the rare case of default, the bank does not require borrowers to sign any legal documents.
- The interest rate on all loans is 11 percent.
- The average loan size is $309.

Source: www.grameen-info.org.

So microlending in the United States is a fairly new phenomenon and as a result the actual number of loans has been fairly low to date. But that is also changing. Recent changes in law have made more money available both for microloans, as well as for technical assistance to microlenders. As a result, in 2010, the number of microloans doubled over the previous year.

One reason you should be excited about this option, aside from the policy decision to increase microlending, is that the actual lending decisions are made based on reasons beyond the pure numbers of your FICO score, bank balance, and collateral levels. Microlenders look at the whole picture, including:

- Your experience
- Your passion
- The market opportunity
- Your sales

It is not surprising that microfinance is emerging as a very viable financing option at this time. Credit has been tight, unemployment has been high, people's credit ratings have taken a hit, and not a few folk have been forced to start a business—whether they wanted to or not. The upshot is that there is a need for capital for microenterprises. No, microloan interest rates are not great, but that is the price you might have to pay.

That microfinance is finally here is the important thing.

THE PLAYERS

Historically, big banks have shied away from making microfinance loans because they are considered to be unprofitable. Accordingly, when looking for a microloan, you need to begin with smaller players, and even some nonprofit players. Microloans are typically available on the local level through community financial institutions. For example, Ryan Fochler was able to finance his pet-sitting business via a microloan from a local nonprofit. That is how these sorts of loans usually work. And, while there are some big names in the tiny loan game, it is all relative. They are "big" by microloan standards, but not by many other measures.

To find a microlender in your area, it is best to begin with a simple Google search of the name of your city or region and "microloan." Beyond that, here are some other good options to check out as you search.

ACCION USA. ACCION is a great group and a significant microloan lender throughout the country. Their own website puts it best:

> *ACCION USA is different from a bank or credit union. ACCION USA is a microfinance organization that lends with the mission of empowering business owners with access to working capital and financial education. We are a recognized leader in small business lending, and a partner you can trust. ACCION USA offers business loans up to $50,000 and financial education throughout the United States. Since 1991, we have specialized in working with small business owners who cannot borrow from the bank due to business type, a short length of time in business, or an insufficient credit history.*

ACCION USA prides itself in helping small businesses get off the ground. Example: One of their clients was Jessica Nickels. Jessica dreamed of owning her own clothing store and making a better life for herself and her two daughters. But bad credit from a divorce and no high school diploma kept this dream out of reach. Jessica was unable to get a conventional loan to start her business.

Then a friend told her about ACCION USA.

Jessica checked ACCION out, applied for a loan, had some consultations with ACCION counselors, and then secured a business loan in the amount of $3,000. She used this money to rent a storefront, get inventory, and launch her business. Jessica says that it was the ACCION loan that made all the difference. "I couldn't have started without the loan," she says. "That's where ACCION came in. They understand." (www.accionusa.org.)

Is it right for you? Here are ACCION's requirements:

- A credit score of 575 or more.
- Have not declared bankruptcy in the past 12 months or foreclosure in the past 24 months.
- Have not had any late rent or mortgage payments in the past 12 months.
- Be up-to-date on all bills.
- Not have more than $3,000 in past-due debt.
- Exhibit steady cash flow and the ability to support monthly loan payments.
- Be able to provide a co-signer, if needed.

> ACCION has a history of quickly responding to crises. After September 11, 2001, ACCION lent millions to businesses in New York City. They did the same thing after Hurricane Katrina.

The SBA. The SBA has been guaranteeing microloans for years. As with its other loan programs, the SBA does not make the loan, but it does make the money available to third-party nonprofit lenders. These lenders then make loans to qualified borrowers. Although the maximum loan amount is $50,000, the average SBA microloan is around $13,000.

Grameen Bank. As a result of the economic turmoil in the past few years, which in turn resulted in an increase in demand for microloans, none other than the Bangladeshi Grameen Bank has opened up shop here in the United States. Operating under the name Grameen America, the microlender has or will open branches in New York, Omaha, San Francisco, Boston, DC, and Charlotte. Loans are adjusted appropriately, but still are micro—$1,500 max.

At the opening of a Grameen America branch in New York, Nobel Prize winner Muhammad Yunus noted, "Wall Street does banking to the world, but it doesn't do banking for its [local] neighbors. We are here to show there's nothing wrong with banking with neighbors." (*Newsweek,* July 19, 2010.)

Kiva. Kiva made its name by offering regular people the chance to loan money to poor, third-world entrepreneurs through the site Kiva.org. Kiva is a great organization that enables people to escape poverty by becoming self-sufficient small business owners.

And now Kiva has come to the United States. Pilot programs began in 2010, and as Premal Shah, president of Kiva, explained, the opening of Kiva offices and the offering of Kiva microloans in the United States was "very timely. People talk about buying local—why not lend local?" (*New York Times,* July 28, 2010.) Kiva does just that. Its loans in the United States work much the same as Kiva loans abroad, with a few differences. Abroad, Kiva borrowers can borrow up to $3,000, whereas here the limit is $10,000 (though the average is around $5,000).

Kiva is also unique in that the model is different than a more traditional microlender wherein a person applies for a loan, meets criteria, meets the staff, and gets the loan. Kiva loans truly are peer-to-peer and as such, the process is different: Entrepreneurs post their biography and business on the Kiva website, and potential lenders, individuals, peruse the site and decide which businesses they would like to invest in. They then donate the money online, but the money does not go directly to the entrepreneur. Instead, it goes to a local microlender, which then disburses the funds and facilitates the repayment of the loan.

For lenders, the important thing to understand is Kiva differs from other P2P sites in that lenders do not make money. According to Kiva, the best you can do is get your money back at 0 percent interest. But that sure is good news for the borrowers.

The idea to bring Kiva to the United States came from Maria Shriver, journalist and wife of then-California Governor Arnold Schwarzenegger. While visiting Kiva offices abroad one year, she wondered whether the Kiva model could be applied back at home. At first, the folks at Kiva were skeptical, but the pain brought on by the Great Recession convinced them that the Kiva model could in fact work in the States and that moreover, it was needed. It has been a resounding success here.

Microlending is growing in popularity and should definitely be on your radar for potential funding options if you fit the criteria. The money is affordable and not impossible to get. To learn more about microfinance, go to the website for the Association of Enterprise Opportunity at www.microenterpriseworks.org.

Bottom Line: If you are looking for a small amount of money for your business, microfinance loans are a great way to go.

CHAPTER **18**

🌀

Royalty and Revenue Sharing

Essential Idea: Presell Products and Share the Revenue

Chester Carlson received a degree in physics from Caltech in 1930 and, even though it was the height of the Great Depression, landed a nice, albeit boring position in the patent office of an electronics company. His job was to assemble and duplicate by hand patent drawings. But given his penchant for inventing, Carlson decided that there had to be a better way. So he began to study photography, the physics of light, and printing. Eventually Carlson learned about photoconductivity—the method by which light affects physical materials.

Carlson decided to see if there was some way to use photoconductivity to capture an image and transfer it onto paper. He eventually was able to perfect a process he called "electrophotography." On October 22, 1938 (10/22/38), in Astoria, Queens, New York, Carlson created a blurry yet legible electrophotographic copy that read, "10.-22.-38 Astoria."

Today, that piece of paper is part of the permanent collection of the Smithsonian.

By the next year, Carlson had scraped together enough money to create a prototype—that didn't work. He then spent the next few years meeting with, demonstrating by hand, and getting turned down by GE, RCA, IBM, and everyone else. These years of fruitless leads led Carlson to financial ruin and divorce. Eventually he found a small, private foundation—the Battelle Memorial Institute—that was interested in his research, and the two parties signed a royalty-sharing agreement in 1944 that allowed Carlson to create a workable prototype by 1945.

Things really changed when, in 1947, a man named Joe Wilson heard about the invention. Wilson owned a small photographic manufacturing business called Haloid. After watching a demonstration of Carlson's electronphotography process, Wilson said, "Of course it's got a million miles to go before it will be marketable. But when it does become marketable, we've got to be in the picture!" Carlson and Wilson signed an agreement that called for Haloid to share the profits and develop the machine.

One of the first things Haloid decided was that the name electrophotography simply had to go. It was too clunky. Several new names were offered: "Kleen Kopy," "Magic Printer," and "Dry Duplicator," to name a few, but none seemed right. Finally, Wilson hired a language professor who suggested that they combine the Greek words for "dry"—*xeros*—and "writing"—*graphein*. And so it was that Carlson's strange and obscure invention came to be known as xerography—hence the Xerox Machine.

ROYALTY FINANCING

Royalty financing is a payment now as an advance against future sales. If you help me develop my Xerox machine now, I will share profits with you down the road. When I got the deal to write this book, I entered into a royalty financing arrangement: I would get a lump sum up-front advance payment to write the book now, and it would be offset by future sales and royalties.

NeurogesX Enters into Royalty Financing Agreement with Cowen Healthcare Royalty Partners: San Mateo, Calif. NeurogesX, Inc. a biopharmaceutical company, announced today that that it has entered into a royalty financing agreement with Cowen Healthcare. Under the terms of the agreement, Cowen will be entitled to receive up to 100% of all royalties and sales milestones due to NeurogesX. After the debt obligation has been fulfilled, payments will revert back to NeurogesX. At any point NeurogesX can retire the Cowen financing and regain access to 100% of its European royalties.

Source: NeurogesX, Inc.

So royalty financing is an arrangement whereby the party seeking financing gets an advance against future sales and those future sales then are used to repay the up-front payment.

Royalty financing has been used by big business for many years, most often in the pharmaceutical, mining, and film industries. You have often heard about a big star taking, say, less up front in exchange for a percentage of the film's profits down the road. That is royalty financing.

In recent years, this form of funding has gained traction in other industries as well because it makes so much sense in the right circumstances. If your business has a steady revenue stream, then it works for everyone if you can sell part of those future earnings in exchange for the lump sum funding you need today.

It may help to think of it this way: In a conventional debt loan arrangement, a lender lends you money that you must repay regularly from whatever source, just as long as you pay. In an equity arrangement, the investor buys into and shares ownership of the business. With factoring, you are selling a specific account that owes you money. But in a revenue sharing arrangement, the lender agrees to take its repayment down the road, sharing the profit on future specific sales. In this way, your repayment options can be much more flexible.

- You can specify which sales and which products apply to the repayment.
- The interest rate may change over time.
- Payments are capped at a certain agreed-upon level.

Here is an example: Let's say that you manufacture toys. You have an opportunity to get your best-selling toy, the Clowniemobile, into a huge new foreign market. The only catch is that you don't have enough capital to ramp up and manufacture enough units. This is where a royalty deal can work well. You would look for and find an investor who is willing to lend you the $1 million you need right now in exchange for, say, 50 percent of the profits over the next three years, or $1.5 million, whichever comes first.

It is a smart deal for the investor because the Clowniemobile has a track record of success, and you have a deal to distribute the product in a virgin market. And it is a great deal for you because you not only get the money you need now, but the payments are capped, and they come out of new sales later. It is less painful that way.

What is even better is that, as indicated, the deal could be structured in any number of ways that suit you. Because you have a valuable asset that you are selling, and because the buyer wants it enough to take payment in the form of revenue sharing down the road, you are in a position of leverage when this sort of deal works. You could ask to make interest-only payments for a few years. Or maybe you want to pay it off quickly, with 100 percent of these sales going to the investor until it is paid in full. That works too. Be creative.

Consider the greatest royalty payment deal in history. Ever. In 1976, the National Basketball Association (NBA) was set to absorb the remaining remnants of the dying American Basketball Association (ABA). There were six ABA teams left, but the NBA decided to adopt only four, leaving the Spirits of St. Louis and the Kentucky Colonels out. The Colonels agreed to a onetime $3.3 million buyout in exchange for disbanding the team. But the owners of the Spirits, brothers Ozzie and Dan Silna, declined.

Instead, they struck a royalty deal that would give them one-seventh of the television revenue of each of the four teams that did get to enter into the NBA: the Denver Nuggets, New Jersey Nets, San Antonio Spurs, and Indiana Pacers. But wait, it gets better. The deal lasts in perpetuity. The language of the deal says that the right *"to receive such revenues shall continue for as long as the NBA or its successors continues in its existence."* The total payments received by the brothers to date now approach a quarter of a billion dollars.

PROS AND CONS

There is a lot to be said for revenue sharing/royalty financing deals:

- You do not have to share equity, board seats, management decisions, or power with an angel or VC. Remember, equity and royalty are different. When an investor takes an equity position, he or she also will have an advisory role. Not so with a royalty deal.

- Because the deal is not a loan, state and federal securities laws are inapplicable, again, as opposed to an equity arrangement.
- Because there is no debt, the advance does not show up as a liability on your balance sheets. It is a "contingent liability."
- Investors can get immediate payment, as, once again, opposed to an equity deal where repayment to the investor may not occur for some time.
- Your shares in your business are not diluted.
- You are not involving friends or family in your business affairs.
- Repayment is made through future sales.
- The investor has a strong and reasonable assurance of repayment.

The downsides are fewer, and less obvious.

- Royalty financing works best with established companies that have a track record of sales. It is much more difficult for a new startup to presell when it does not yet have a revenue stream.
- You are still taking on debt and one of your main avenues for growth—future sales—will be earmarked toward repayment of that debt.
- Some royalty deals can take years to pay off, and therefore may end up being much more expensive than a bank loan.
- Investors may not like that their income potential from the deal will be capped. When a VC invests in a hot startup in exchange for a 30 percent position, that 30 percent could eventually equal almost anything. Not so with a royalty financing agreement.
- If you default, you may lose, big time. Investors' investments are sometimes secured by your best assets in a royalty deal.

How not to do a royalty deal: The country of Madagascar, one of the poorest in the world, entered into a mining royalty deal in 2008 that would net it but 1 percent in royalty payments from the mine for a minimum of 20 years.

ADDITIONAL POINTS TO CONSIDER

When considering a royalty funding agreement, it is important that there be a limit on the amount of money that can be repaid to the lender; you do not want to pay some percentage in perpetuity, like the NBA does.

Additionally, royalty deals are not good for businesses that have tight profit margins. The reason, of course, is that your repayments come out of your profits. As such, if profits are squeaked out in your business, adding an additional layer of overhead to your already thin margins can tip the balance in the wrong direction. Be careful of that.

Finally, you want to be sure that the pricing on whatever product you choose to sell against is elastic enough that you can still make money on it, despite the royalty payment. You don't want the royalty deal to turn that product into a loss leader.

Bottom Line: Revenue sharing and royalty agreements can be a great source of income for your business as long as you can afford to share your profits down the road.

CHAPTER 19

Supplier, Wholesaler, and Franchisor Financing

Essential Idea: Work with Your Supply Chain to Get the Funding You Need

When Arnold Goldstein decided to open his first shoestring business, he had little money but big plans. His vision was to create a wholesale warehouse open to the public (back in the day, long before such stores like Costco were popular). He would call it "Discount City." Goldstein eventually did create that store, and 12 more just like it, but only after using some very creative funding methods.

As Goldstein explains it in his great book, *Starting on a Shoestring*, when he opened the door to his first Discount City, "the mountains of merchandise were jam-packed on a wide array of used fixtures, painted nauseating green to hide their disparate origins. To my left were the $3.98 garbage cans and to my right were the crates of six-fingered back scratchers direct from Taiwan at the incredible 49-cent price. Wherever I looked there were bargains galore, hustled and conned on credit from every corner of the map." (John Wiley & Sons, 2002.)

Goldstein says that the original Discount City opened with "$120,000 of unpaid-for merchandise that was heaped on $20,000 in fully mortgaged fixtures sitting on retail space with three months' deferred rent." Not only that, but he boasts that although the original store "came to life owing everybody for everything" and was built on "a financial house of cards," he nevertheless was able to grow it to a baker's dozen of stores within three years, grossing $6 million in sales.

"Best of all, it was started on a shoestring with only $2,600 of my own cash."

Wow.

The story of how Arnold Goldstein accomplished that is the story of how you can do it too. When we speak of using supplier and wholesaler financing for a business, we are talking about a combination of in-kind contributions, trade credit, direct loans, and creative financing. This is definitely the shoestring financing chapter of the book.

SUPPLIER AND WHOLESALER FINANCING

When people first learn of this funding option, they are usually surprised. It cannot really be true that a supplier would be willing to lend you cash money for your business, right? Wrong. Under the right circumstances, with the right supplier and a deal that makes sense, you absolutely can get a supplier to pony up some money in support of your business. As Goldstein says, "Suppliers can be a generous bunch."

Let's look at those three conditions:

1. *The right supplier.* It is unrealistic to think that a large, nationwide supplier would lend you money for your business. Why should they? They don't need your business, and in any case, a large corporation is going to have very rigid guidelines and policies that will forbid it from lending money anyway, especially to a small business, and especially to a startup small business.

   Instead, what you are looking for is a smaller, local supplier or wholesaler. One who really wants your business.

2. *The right circumstances.* Let's say that you want to create your own version of Discount City; how much business might that give one of your main suppliers over the course of a year? Let's say it's $100,000 a year. A six-figure client is a great client. And that is why a supplier just might lend you $10,000 or so. They want your business, and if lending you some money to help you get your business off the ground means

creating a lucrative, long-term, six-figure customer, it makes sense. That is called "the right circumstances." Would you do it if you were in their shoes? Exactly.

> Peter Hassan started his business, Henrick Interior Studio, with almost nothing. "I had the carpet down, lights up, fixtures in place, and a sign over the front door. What I didn't have was inventory—or the money or credit to buy it." But what Hassan did have were smarts and chutzpah. Hassan did some research and realized that there were 4,000 wholesalers and distributors who had products he could sell. As Goldstein relates in *Starting on a Shoestring*, Hassan says, "That gave me 4,000 chances to succeed." Using a variety of creative credit conditions and deferred deals, Hassan was able to get almost $100,000 worth of product in the store within two months.

3. *The right deal.* You cannot ask for a lot of money, and you cannot ask for a long-term loan. The loan has to make economic and business sense to the supplier. For them, it is a means to an end.

Assuming that you have the right supplier, deal, and circumstances in mind, how do you get someone to say yes? Here is what Arnold Goldstein suggests:

1. First, begin by getting a credit rating: Get listed at Dun & Bradstreet. You won't have a credit rating to start with, but you will at least be listed.

2. Get some credit references: Personal references are fine. Have a bank reference ready too.

3. Look legit: You need a real store or office, stationery, printed purchase orders, website, a dynamite business plan, and a corporate name—the whole enchilada. Look serious if you want to be taken seriously.

4. Start with the sales reps: Salespeople want to sell to you. Pitch them your plan and explain how a small loan from their company will secure your future and your future patronage of their business. You will be forever in their debt (figuratively, of course). The salespeople will bump you up the chain of command to the right person with whom to speak.

5. Have a solid plan: Explain what the money will be used for exactly, and how it will be repaid.

6. Have some skin in the game: The supplier will want to know what you are putting into the venture, aside from your sweat equity. Be honest. If you are donating equipment or material, say so. If you are tapping credit cards, so be it. Your commitment helps your cause.

Before a supplier will agree to lending you money, they will want to visit your business, contact your references, and make sure you have a very good shot at repaying the loan. The key to success is preparation. Having a good idea is not enough. You need to make a solid presentation that explains how your business using their loan will benefit their bottom line. If you can actually get some preorders and then explain that you need financing to fill those orders, even better.

When structuring a supplier loan, keep these points in mind:

- Make sure that it is your company taking out the loan, and not you personally.
- How much interest will you have to pay? Remember, everything is negotiable.
- How long is the term? You need to crunch some numbers to see how much you can afford to repay every month.
- Be picky. If you can get one supplier interested, you can probably get others.

Does this plan really work? Here is what Arnold Goldstein says in *Starting on a Shoestring*: "Discount City was helped along by a $5,000 working capital loan from its photofinishing supplier and $3,000 from its tobacco jobber. Why be embarrassed to ask? These suppliers now sell over $800,000 a year to Discount City stores."

TRADE CREDIT

Obviously, Goldstein did not open Discount City just by getting some supplier loans. He also was able to establish a great deal of trade credit (sometimes known as vendor financing). While trade credit is not cash per se, it is nonetheless one of the largest sources of in-kind capital in the world. It is a basic building block for any business looking to grow and/or establish a business credit profile.

Establishing trade credit offers several benefits to your business. First is that it allows you to buy the materials you need to run your business and stock your shelves. Second, it helps to create a financial profile for your company. In addition, trade credit is often cheaper than using credit cards or other borrowed money.

Establishing trade credit. Like regular personal credit, the more business trade credit you establish, the more that will become available to you, and at better terms. You begin by starting small. Look to establish credit first with:

- The phone company
- Office supply stores
- Other small suppliers

What you are looking to do is establish an "on account" or "open account" arrangement that allows you to buy on credit. If you are able to pay the amount off in full every month, your positive business credit profile will grow quickly.

There are also a few bank-related ways to build trade credit:

- First, open a business credit card with a small credit line and again, try to pay it off in full every month.
- Open a business savings account at your bank and inquire about taking out a small passbook loan secured by the account. The bank likes it because it is a loan with fees for you to pay, and is a secured loan to boot. For you, that the bank will report your good payments to the credit reporting agencies every month is even better.
- If you are willing to offer a personal guarantee, the bank may open a business line of credit for you too.

What not to do: Use your own personal credit cards to pay business expenses and debts. If you do that, then you end up commingling your personal and business finances and credit, and you will never establish business credit.

After a year or two of paying these open accounts and loans regularly, you will find that your business will have a solid credit rating and access to far more trade and other credit.

FRANCHISOR FINANCING

If you are looking to buy a franchise, then a unique option available only to you is that of franchisor financing. According to the International Franchising Association, most franchisors offer some type of financing, meaning the franchisor will assist in financing at least part of a franchisee's obligation.

The types of loan vary, with some franchisors making direct loans to the franchisee, while others (and the majority) offer access to third-party lenders knowledgeable about the specific franchise and its financial requirements. Other franchisor alternatives, aside from direct lending, include loan guarantees or working capital.

> To see whether the franchise you are interested in offers any sort of financing, review the Franchise Disclosure Document (FDD). Item 10 discusses relevant financing options.

The actual process of obtaining franchisor financing is usually just like the one you follow when applying for any other type of financing. You will need to present the franchisor (if it is a direct loan) or its finance partner (if it is a third-party loan) your business plan, credit history, collateral options, other such documents, and loan requirements. Note: It is very rare that you would be able to obtain 100 percent financing for a franchise.

Bottom Line: Whether it is direct lending, third-party financing, or trade credit, another rich and often untapped source of business funding comes from working with your supply chain.

CHAPTER 20

Seller Financing

Essential Idea: Looking to Buy a Business? Get the Current Owner to Finance Some or All of the Purchase

Dan Dubinsky (name and some minor facts changed for privacy) has owned a couple of auto body shops for 20 years, and for at least the past three, has planned on selling the business and retiring to the South of France with his wife. Dubinsky figures that the business is worth about $250,000 and that that would make a nice nest egg, along with his other investments.

But the changing economy shifted his plans.

Dubinsky put his business up for sale, and to entice buyers, offered to finance up to 40 percent of the purchase. Although he is not thrilled with taking $100,000 less up front, he also knows that it makes the sale of his business much more likely. Dubinsky realizes that he will have a much better chance of finding a qualified buyer in this climate if the purchase is made easier by seller financing.

Certainly this is not a new or radical idea. By some estimates, up to 75 percent of all small business sales include some degree of financing on the part of sellers. The reason is obvious: Most buyers do not have the capital resources necessary to purchase outright, or even finance a majority of, a successful small business. These days, banks do not offer anything close to the 100 percent financing they offered for business purchases back in the late 1990s. And so between tighter bank restrictions and less fluid buyers, owners are increasingly forced to offer partial (and sometimes whole) financing in order to facilitate a sale.

In Dubinsky's case, he figures that a good buyer should be able to come up with $50,000 down. A bank should finance another $100,000, and he will take the remaining $100,000 using a five-year balloon note. It works for everyone. The buyer gets in putting only 20 percent down, the bank does not have a lot of exposure, and Dubinsky gets to sell his business and retire, while also receiving some steady income for the next five years and then a lump sum payment.

SELLER FINANCING

Buying an existing business is usually a very good idea, for several reasons. For one, it is less risky. You can review the books of the business and get a pretty good idea as to how much money you can expect to make. That simply is not true with a new startup. Also, there is a built-in customer base. That is great. Additionally, you do not have to spend years creating a reputation and brand; that goodwill is already something established and something you will be purchasing. Finally, you can usually get the present owner to stick around a bit and teach you the ropes, so the learning curve is less steep. All in all, buying an established business is usually a pretty smart entrepreneurial move.

That said, such businesses can be expensive and so the question arises: How do you get your purchase funded? That is where seller financing comes in. And as the story of Dan Dubinsky proves, sellers today are willing to finance at least part of the sale. That makes your job that much easier.

It's a win-win. Obviously, for you, it makes purchasing the business much easier. It also means that whatever oral promises the seller makes (to spend some time after the sale helping you learn how to run the business, for instance) must be done since the seller cannot risk angering you. Their financing is your assurance that the deal should proceed as agreed upon. But equally for sellers, the reasons are clear: By helping to finance the sale, they can get a better price and facilitate a faster sale.

SELLER FINANCING DEALS EXPLAINED

Seller financing is where an owner of a business agrees to carry a promissory note as whole or (far more often) partial payment for the sale of the business. This sort of financing is well-known in the real estate world where the owner of a home agrees to "carry the paper" for the buyer so that the buyer can more easily qualify for a conventional loan for the remainder. The homeowner's note is usually recorded as a second mortgage and is paid off in due time. The same idea is at play with owner financing in the sale of a business. The owner carries the paper and is paid off over time.

Seller financing can occur in all sorts of situations:

- Where the purchase price is so high that an all-cash purchase is difficult. Typically, this is where the business is worth $100,000 or more.
- Where the seller is very motivated to sell.
- Where the seller likes the buyer but the buyer does not have the means to purchase the business.

There are, of course, plenty of other reasons and situations where the seller might finance the sale of his or her own business.

How much should you expect the seller to finance and what might the deal look like? It really all depends upon the parties involved. The seller might finance anywhere from 25 to 75 percent of the purchase, and yes, 100 percent deals are possible, albeit uncommon. The seller will usually hold out for more of his asking price if he agrees to carry a note. The interest rate you should expect to pay should be near the going rate, although 10 percent interest is not an uncommon legal rate to pay. The note usually does not last more than seven years; five years is more common. You should expect to make payments monthly, with a possible balloon payment due upon maturity of the note.

> Although seller-financed notes usually do not last more than seven years, that changes if real estate is involved in the purchase of the business. In that case, you should expect the maturity date to be much later.

WHAT'S IN IT FOR THE SELLER?

You may not think that an owner of a business would want to finance its sale to a buyer who otherwise could not qualify . . . and you would be right. Sellers don't usually want to do this and only agree to it when they have no choice. Usually, a seller will try to sell the business the old-fashioned way first. If successful, great, but if not, they become like the homeowner whose house has been on the market too long: they want to get out and look for creative solutions and new options.

That's where you come in.

By offering the owner a way out, a chance to sell the business if they carry some paper, you put yourself in position to kill two birds with one stone: You get financing to buy a business and the owner gets to sell their business. You become a solution to their problem. Is it perfect? No, for the seller, of course not. But your offer to buy with owner financing is probably more than they have right now, so it is something.

Of course, you have to offer more than just a warm body. Consider what the seller wants: she wants to get out of the business, to take the money and run. So you have to show her how working with you helps her accomplish her goals. You will need:

- Experience
- A vision for the business
- Some other financing (hopefully)
- An offer that makes sense
- A viable and timely exit strategy for the seller

Aside from an actual sale, another benefit of owner financing for the current owner is that it should create a faster sale. By making it easier for the buyer to get into the business, by acting as the buyer's bank in essence, the seller ensures that the sale of the business can occur much more quickly. Banks can sometimes work slow. Banks require documentation. Banks may say no. By becoming the bank, the seller can make things happen pronto.

Offering financing will also enable the owner to offer the business for sale to many more people. There will be more action because more people will be able to qualify. If owners hold out for only those people who can either pay cash or get a conventional loan, they will limit their sale options significantly.

> Business brokers may have a role in the transaction as well. Business brokers get paid when the business sells and as such, have a vested interest in any sort of deal that can help facilitate that. The broker will likely advise the owner that carrying part of the paper will help sell the business.

Additionally, the seller may agree to seller financing because it makes a lot of sense for other reasons too:

- The seller (and buyer) will save in closing costs if a bank is only minimally involved.
- The seller should receive almost all of her asking price.
- The seller should get an ongoing interest payment that is typically more than she could otherwise get from another investment.
- The seller knows that the business is viable and therefore that the loan is a smart and safe one to make.
- If there are any problems with the business or property, the seller can negotiate an "as-is" provision, which would be hard to do with more conventional financing.

Are there risks involved? Of course! This is business, after all. There are always risks. The main one is that the buyer will default on the loan and the seller will be forced to repossess a business she no longer wants. That is a real risk and always a possibility. But a seller can diminish the likelihood of that happening by doing some due diligence. The seller must check out the buyer as much as the buyer must check out the seller and the business. The seller must become comfortable with the buyer's ability to successfully run the business. The seller must do a background and credit check on the buyer and secure the deal with collateral.

While the risks are real, they should not become a deterrent. For the small business owner, the benefits usually outweigh the detriments. Yes, the owner will have some of his or her money tied up in the business for a few years, but if done correctly and to the right buyer, the sale of the business using seller financing should realize the seller a nice profit and quick sale.

WHAT'S IN IT FOR THE BUYER?

Of course the first thing is that owner financing should enable you to get into a business that you might not otherwise be able to get into. That is huge. But the benefits to you go far beyond that.

First of all, that the owner is willing to finance some or all of the sale should be of comfort to you as it is proof that this really is a good business; otherwise, the seller would not finance it. Financing a lemon is a sure way to get a deal breached since you would have little incentive to keep making payments on a business that loses money. If the seller believes enough in this business to be willing to finance it, you should believe in it too. Seller financing proves you are likely making a smart choice.

Of course, seller financing will also allow you to get into the business with little or no money down, and that in turn should enable you to retain what cash you do have to run the business. Better to have your money in your hands than the ex-owner's hands. He will get his share down the road, when you can better afford it.

In addition, since a common clause in an owner-financing arrangement is that the owner will stick around and help and teach during the transition time, you will have a great shoulder to lean on. Learning about the business from the person who ran it successfully for many years is the sort of business home run that does not come around very often. It truly is a unique and valuable factor.

FINDING A SELLER WHO IS WILLING TO FINANCE A BUSINESS

It actually may not be as hard as it sounds. You would look in all of the places you normally would when looking to buy a business, only this time you would additionally be on the lookout for an owner that offers to "carry the paper," or who is "motivated," or who says "financing is available." Those are the magic words.

The places to look include:

- Craigslist ("Businesses for sale")
- The Businesses for Sale or Business Opportunities classified section of your Sunday paper
- The back of specific, industry-related magazines
- Websites like BusinessBuySell.com

- Google searches
- Business brokers

THE SELLER FINANCING DEAL

Seller financing deals are usually fairly creative and can be flexible enough to account for any contingency or issue the buyer or seller cares to include. The deal will include the following provisions:

- Sale price
- Amount of down payment
- Interest rate
- Length of time on the note
- Terms of any balloon clause
- Specific description of what is being bought and sold, including: real estate, goodwill, inventory, other property, customer lists, intellectual property, stock, and signage
- Employment clauses: What will happen to current employees (are they guaranteed a job and if so, for how long?)

Additionally, the seller will want to include some or all of the following provisions:

- Security: Something needs to collateralize the loan, either a significant business asset or even the buyer's home.
- A personal guarantee on the part of the buyer.
- Other remedies in case of default.
- A life or disability policy naming the seller as the beneficiary until the note is paid off.

> Another form of security for the ex-owner is something called a stock pledge. Here, the buyer forms a new corporation with the ex-owner as the majority shareholder. Provisions in the by-laws give the seller the right to force the new owner to make all payments due under the note and even gives the ex-owner the right to bring in new management in the case of a default. Just this provision alone usually means that the note is never defaulted upon.

The buyer will want these provisions:

- Seller assistance: The buyer may want the seller to stay on for a certain length of time to assist in training.
- No compete: The buyer may want the seller to agree not to compete against the business for a certain length of time.
- Customer protection: Similarly, the buyer may want the seller to agree not to poach any of the business's existing customers.
- The buyer may also want a graduated payment or interest rate, where the amount he or she owes starts low and increases over time.

Of course, all of this must be worked out with your own lawyer. You absolutely must be represented by counsel in any seller financing business sale.

Bottom Line: Seller financing is a great opportunity for a seller to more easily sell a business and for a buyer to get in easier. It should be a win-win.

CHAPTER 21

Business Plan Competitions and Other Contests

Essential Idea: Enter Your Business or Business Plan into a Contest to Win Big Money to Fund Your Business

Economically depressed Washington, DC, decided that one way to spur development and promote entrepreneurship in the city would be to have a business plan competition. According to Steve Moore, the president and CEO of the Washington DC Economic Partnership (WDCEP), "Small business can thrive here. We want to be known as a place where entrepreneurs bring their ideas and make them real." (PR Newswire, March 29, 2010.) So WDCEP teamed up with some partners and launched a business plan competition. To qualify, a business needed to compete in a series of oral presentations against other teams.

The winner that year was a business called Affinity Labs, a company that manages a shared cooperative workspace for small businesses, entrepreneurs, nonprofits, and startups. At Affinity Labs, "members develop the services, clients, partners, vendors, processes and infrastructure they need to succeed on their own. Think of it as shared office space meets incubator meets entrepreneurial clubhouse." (www.AffinityLabs.com.)

Affinity Labs competed against 40 other DC businesses over two months and ended up in the finals against three other strong teams. Each finalist gave a 30-minute pitch before a panel that included business owners, VCs, government officials, professors, and graduate business students. In the end, the panel decided that Affinity Labs had the best idea and plan to spur development in our nation's capital.

Their winnings? A cool $100,000.

HOW BUSINESS PLAN COMPETITIONS WORK

There are many business plan competitions all across the country, and although most are collegiate and geared toward MBA students, there are also many that are open to the general public, as in the previous example. Either way, the idea is the same: Along with all of the other teams in the competition, you pitch your business and plan to a panel of judges through a series of competitions and the winner walks off with some money and in-kind contributions.

> Business plan competitions first emerged at the University of Texas in the 1980s. Two Texas MBA students wanted to create a business school competition akin to the moot court competitions law schools offered. The first competition for their brainchild, the "Moot Corp.," was for Texas MBA students only, in 1984. The idea quickly spread to top business schools like Harvard, the Wharton School of Business, and the London Business School and are now found around the world. In 2010, the original Austin-based Texas University competition was attended by 40 teams from 12 countries.

The purpose of a business plan competition is twofold. First, it is to seek out, find, and reward the best businesses and business plans in the region. The hope is to encourage entrepreneurs and help facilitate their success. In so doing, the winning businesses, the host of the competition, and the region all benefit as new and vibrant businesses are born. A secondary purpose of such competitions is to encourage entrepreneurship generally. By hosting a competition, publicizing it, and encouraging participation in it, the host group fosters a more entrepreneurial community.

As such, participants may expect to get plenty of help along the way as they proceed through the competition, since it is most certainly not just about winning the money. By entering a business plan competition, you can expect to receive mentoring, networking opportunities, business education, and assistance with your pitch.

The specific experience might look like this:

1. *Entry.* You find a local business plan competition that fits your business or business plan, you assemble your team, and you fill out the entry form, pay the fee (typically no more than $100), and enter.
2. *Screening round.* This is the initial review of each business plan and team. You give your best pitch, explain the genius of your plan, business, and team to the judges, and cross your fingers. Expect to be grilled. If successful you move on to the next round with, say, half of the original teams.
3. *Semifinals.* You may have to pitch your full plan again, or possibly give an abbreviated elevator pitch. Expect to be grilled again.
4. *Finals.* A few teams, usually four, make it to the final round of pitches. Your final presentation will last 30 minutes or so with the pitch and judges' question-and-answer session included.
5. *Winner.* There is, of course, the grand prize winner that takes home the big bucks, but there are also runners-up who get money too, and winners in different categories.

There are all sorts of benefits that come with winning the competition aside from the money. In addition to the actual funding, winners in various categories might also receive administrative support, incubator space, ongoing business coaching, and legal and other services. They also get a lot of great press. Beyond that, the contacts they make often also prove invaluable. Indeed, as investors are involved in business plan competitions, and as they are always looking for a good idea—whether those ideas turn out to be the winners or not—not a few startups find their angels at business plan competitions.

FINDING BUSINESS PLAN COMPETITIONS

So this probably sounds like a pretty intriguing idea to you, and it should. The chance to fund your business by winning a competition and receiving funding (that you don't have to repay!) is pretty special. That you will meet the players in your community is even better.

One challenge you may encounter is that, as indicated previously, many of these competitions are for business school students. But there are two things to keep in mind:

1. "Many" is not "all." There are plenty of competitions that are not for students.
2. The student competitions do not often require that all members of the team be students. You can team up with a student team, or get a student to join your team. That is perfectly acceptable. It may also be that it will suffice if you are simply an alumnus of the school.

Finding local business plan competitions is not difficult. Begin by checking out your local university, especially its graduate business school. Also check with your local SBDC and SCORE office. They are conduits for entrepreneurship news. And of course, a Google search of the relevant terms will also lead you in the right direction. One final suggestion: Many venture capital firms are now sponsoring their own business plan competitions. Check that out too.

"The Clean Tech Business Competition Deadline is May 30. The Clean Tech Open is a business plan competition that will provide more than $1 million in prizes for early-stage clean technology startups. Over the past three years, the Clean Tech Open has helped more than one hundred startups raise more than $125 million in funding." (www.cleantechopen.com.)

Some of these competitions offer six-figure payouts to the winner, but many are not as well funded. A typical winner may get $25,000 in cash and $25,000 in services. And although money is the name of the game in this book, do not overlook the other extras that come from just entering into a business plan completion: You will meet some great people interested in what you are doing, you will get to hone your pitch skills, and you will get valuable feedback on your idea.

HOW TO WIN A BUSINESS PLAN COMPETITION

What are the secrets to winning one of these prestigious events? Needless to say, you will need to have a business idea and plan that fills a market need, one that is unique and that resonates. You will need to be able to give a crackerjack presentation.

Here are some other salient points to remember:

Understand the difference. A business plan competition business plan is not necessarily the same as a real-world business plan. Here you have only 15 minutes or so and a short PowerPoint presentation to make your pitch. Hit the highlights. Deal with the core, essential elements. Don't drill down too deep. Topics to hit: size of the market, the unique opportunity, the competition, and your "secret sauce."

Remember, there's no business like show business. This is not only a competition, it's a public competition. Don't read your presentation and don't memorize it. Be interesting and pithy.

Have a great idea. Judges look for unique ideas that have the potential for high growth. You want to show them how you can leverage what you already have and, with a little help, take things to a new level. Having a patent or some other intellectual property helps.

Be compelling. What you are doing in a business plan competition is showing how your idea is a viable solution to a real market problem. Be charming and smart, yes, but also creative and memorable. Make a compelling case for you, your team, and the business. And yes, it is indeed a tall order.

Have a great team. As with venture capitalists, judges at business plan competitions give close scrutiny to the team you have assembled. Can they pull it off? Do they have the requisite experience and know-how? How are their presentation skills? And internally, remember that you want a team that gets along well with one another.

Deal with feedback and questions. You will get both. Judges will take into account your willingness to listen and learn. Getting defensive and arguing do not help your cause.

In 2005, a team from UCLA won the Rice University business plan competition, and with it, $100,000. But the real prize came down the road when some VCs in attendance decided to invest $1.1 million in the nascent company. Other Rice University winner stats:

- A total of 270 teams have competed at the Rice Business Plan competition since 2001. Thirty-five percent are successful and now in operation.
- Previous competitors have raised over $75 million.
- Of the 42 teams that participated in the 2009 competition, 79 percent launched their business. Seventy-two percent are still in business.

Source: www.alliance.rice.edu.

OTHER COMPETITIONS

Similar to business plan competitions, there are a host of other business/entrepreneurship/startup competitions that essentially seek to do the same thing: find and reward the best businesses with the best ideas. Google "startup competitions."

Some of the ones you may want to check out are:

The MIT $100K Entrepreneurship Challenge. Since 1989, the Massachusetts Institute of Technology (MIT) has hosted a series of yearly entrepreneurship contests, including an elevator pitch contest in which competitors have 60 seconds to woo judges. The top prize is $10,000. Another one of the contests is the Tweet Pitch, or "Twitch." Contestants use 140 characters or less to win $500. (www.mit100k.org.)

The GE Ecomagination Challenge. "A $200 million innovation experiment where businesses, entrepreneurs, innovators and students share their best ideas on how to build the next-generation power grid." (http://challenge.ecomagination.com.)

Amazon Web Services Start-Up Challenge. Winners receive $50,000 in cash and $50,000 in AWS service credits.

The Global Social Entrepreneurship Competition (GSEC). This is an international social venture plan competition, where teams propose commercially viable businesses that work to reduce poverty in the developing world.

The Mass Challenge. This is an annual global startup competition in Massachusetts, although "anyone can enter, with any idea, from anywhere in the world" since the goal is to "catalyze a global startup renaissance." Winners partake in a $1 million cash pool, mentorship, and free office space. (www.masschallenge.org.)

There are literally thousands of such business plan and entrepreneurial competitions held every year. By finding one or more that fit your business, you can go a long way toward securing the funding you need.

Bottom Line: Business plan and other competitions can be an excellent way to not only receive business funding, but obtain other valuable resources as well.

SECTION VI

In-Kind Contributions

CHAPTER 22

Business Incubators

Essential Idea: Seed Money, Free Help, Mentorship, and In-Kind Services Can Take You over the Top

What's that you say? You have a few old cell phones lying around the house but don't know what to do with them? You and millions of others. If we lived in San Diego, we could drop them off at a green ecoATM kiosk to be recycled. And if the test of these clever kiosks goes as well as expected—one of the backers is the company that rolled out the uber-successful Redbox DVD rental boxes—we soon won't need to live in San Diego to use them.

The ecoATM is a business born in a nonprofit high-tech business incubator in Southern California called EvoNexus. Like almost all similar business incubators, the EvoNexus incubator offers its startups a wide range of services at low or no cost: office space, support services, business coaching, legal and accounting assistance, networking, and much more. The idea is to provide all of the vital services that a typical startup might need, for 24 months, thereby allowing the new company to concentrate more on successfully launching their product or service and less on the gritty, day-to-day minutiae of operations.

EvoNexus is a fairly new business incubator and, like almost all such endeavors, is a public-private partnership. In this case, it is sponsored by San Diego Regional Economic Development Corporation and companies like PricewaterhouseCoopers. Its purpose is to foster entrepreneurship, high-tech business development, and economic growth in the region.

ecoATM "graduated" from the EvoNexus program in less than a year and in the process raised more than $10 million in venture capital. In addition, as explained to *San Diego Metropolitan Magazine*, "the company also found help with insurance, shipping, and writing an iPhone application." And the free rent at the incubator was another bonus. As CEO Tom Tullie said, "investors want you to be cheap but they don't want you to look cheap [and therefore, being housed in the incubator] made us look bigger and better." (*San Diego Metropolitan Magazine*, October 21, 2010.)

The future for the company looks bright indeed. As their website says, "Given the enormous underserved worldwide demand for used mobile phones and other electronics, and the enormous and perpetually growing cache of these devices cluttering the homes of US consumers, a rare opportunity exists to build an enterprise which benefits consumers, retailers, OEM's, and the environment alike."

Welcome to the world of business incubators.

BUSINESS INCUBATORS

Starting a business is difficult. There is a lot to know and do, it is exhausting and expensive, and there are many moving parts. On top of that, as you know only too well, money is usually tight. How do you balance the financial needs of renting space, hiring staff, building a brand, and launching a business? It's almost like deciding which of your children deserves to be fed—they all need to eat.

That's where business incubators come in. Business incubators are collaborative programs designed to help new startups with some of the most vexing issues they face. By providing workspace, support services, networking opportunities, and yes, sometimes even money, business incubators kick-start worthy businesses.

> Do business incubators work? You bet. According to a study conducted by the University of Michigan and the National Business Incubation Association (NBIA) entitled *Business Incubation Works*, an amazing 87 percent of business incubation graduates stay in business.

Business incubators are usually funded and run by some consortium of local governments, private enterprise, trade associations, local entrepreneurs, and universities. But that said, business incubators are not all the same. Typically, different regions with different industries create incubators around those industries. You will find high-tech incubators in the Silicon Valley and agricultural incubators in the Midwest. You can find incubators that cover everything from tourism to healthcare, green technology, Internet services, food, fashion, and much more.

For example:

- The Innovation Depot in Birmingham, Alabama, is a 140,000-square-foot facility housed in a former Sears department store. It is funded by the University of Alabama, the Birmingham business community, leading foundations, and the City of Birmingham. It focuses on the development of startups in industries as varied as biotechnology, IT, and service.
- Idea Village in New Orleans offers a variety of programs. Its nine-month "Entrepreneur Challenge" allows participating startups to receive coaching, attend weekly workshops, and get help from a team of MBA students. In addition, the program offers access to development grants and shared workspace. As of the time of this writing, the program had supported almost 600 startups.
- 8ninths is a private incubator in Seattle started by two former Microsoft employees. The incubator invests up to $250,000 in Internet software ventures that can be "validated without a big upfront investment."

And as varied as the incubators are, so too are the different services they provide. The list of potential business incubation services includes:

- Workspace
- Warehousing and manufacturing space
- Clerical and secretarial assistance
- Shared computers, fax machines, and other equipment
- Marketing assistance
- Networking opportunities and mentorship
- Product development services
- Legal, financial, and accounting help
- Access to financing partners, angel investors, and VCs
- General business and technical support

> Business incubation in the United States began when Joseph Mancuso opened the Batavia Industrial Center in a warehouse in Batavia, New York, in 1959. By 1980, the number of incubators in the country had grown to only 12. Today, however, the NBIA estimates that there are about 1,500 business incubators in North America. For more information on business incubators, contact the NBIA at 614-593-4331, or visit www.nbia.org.

Of course if you are reading this book, you would prefer a business incubator that offers funding as part of its package. Welcome to the club. The fact is some do, many do not, and those that do are more difficult to get into. To find an incubator that offers funding, your Google search should include terms like "seed funding," "financing," and "access to capital."

But even if you are not near, or cannot get into, an incubator that offers seed funding, do not despair. Remember, when it comes to getting your business funded, money can look many different ways. Sure, getting actual funding is what you want, but free rent and the other services listed earlier are not insignificant. You would spend your funding on many of those things anyway, so getting them for free (or practically free) should be considered the next best thing and a boon to your business.

Indeed, if there is anything bad to say about incubators, it is this: If you are fortunate enough to get into one, you will get spoiled. Subsidized rent, contacts, excellent advice, and free assistance are hard to beat. And because the point of a business incubator is to launch new businesses, you will eventually have to move out; sooner rather than later you won't be the new kid on the block any longer; someone else will.

GETTING INTO AN INCUBATOR

Not surprisingly, getting accepted into a business incubation program is no easy task. There is a lot of competition for one of the few coveted spots. Getting accepted into an incubator is not unlike getting accepted into any prestigious program. You have to apply for admission and impress the judges. That said, because the very purpose of a business incubator is to foster the growth of new startups, you do not need to have a lot of money or customers to be accepted. What you do need is a great idea, a viable path, and a good business plan.

Because different incubators focus on different sorts of business, it is impossible to state specifically what different incubators look for and what the selection process may consist of. It may be as easy as an application and an interview, or as complicated as a stringent multiround screening process.

That said, it is safe to say that any business incubator wants not only a business or entrepreneur that has a good chance of succeeding, but one that can be taken over the top by the assistance of the incubator; that is, the incubation process will be the tipping point to their success. Incubators also want businesses that will bring jobs to the area. They want businesses that will help spur industry and grow the reputation of both the region and the incubator. Other goals that the incubator may have, besides fostering a new business, include:

- Diversifying the local economy.
- Specializing the local economy.
- Economic revitalization.

The upshot is that incubators look to bring in early-stage companies with growth potential that really could use the help of the incubator.

> The NBIA estimates that in 2005, business incubators in the United States assisted more than 27,000 startup companies. These businesses employed more than 100,000 workers and generated more than $17 billion in annual revenue.

HOW IT WORKS

Here are two examples of how two very different business incubators operate:

TechStars is a private (not quasi-public like most) three-month business incubation program run out of four cities: Boston, Boulder, New York, and Seattle. The program accepts only about 10 businesses per city per year, although hundreds apply.

The incubator chooses companies that propose "products that solve real problems or create meaningful innovations." TechStars especially looks for businesses with a great team and as such rarely accepts companies with only one founder. As they say, "[One of] the best things you can do to strengthen your application [is to] round out your team with people who have business, technical, and other necessary skills." (www.techstars.org.)

Companies that are accepted into the program receive $6,000 in seed funding per owner (maximum $18,000 total). As TechStars puts it, their purpose is to help participants "get their startup funded and off the ground while learning from the best."

If you get accepted into this incubator, you would get, aside from the seed money:

- *Advice and mentoring.* During the intense three months of the program, participants have access to an array of talented mentors. "About two or three times per week, we will organize an informal dinner and invite our mentors to speak on a relevant topic. These will be presented as appropriate by highly successful entrepreneurs, angel investors, legal experts, venture capitalists, investment bankers, etc."
- *Introductions and connections.* "At the end of the program, each company also has the opportunity to pitch during an investor event that we organize. Usually there are more than 200 VCs and angel investors in attendance."
- *Office space and related services, if so desired.* You do not have to be based in any of the four cities to participate in the program. "We provide working and meeting spaces, as well as a nice lounge all with super fast and reliable wireless Internet access. Still, many of our founders choose to work from their apartments or local coffee shops. It's up to you."
- *A partner.* Most business incubators do not seek an equity position in the companies they help, but some do, and TechStars is one of those. In exchange for all of the aforementioned, TechStars receives a 6 percent equity stake in your new company.

Described next is a nontechnical, more small business–oriented incubator:

The mission of the Thurston County Small Business Incubator in Olympia, Washington, is to "create jobs by helping entrepreneurs and small businesses access resources they need for growth and long term success." The incubator is a public-private partnership funded by the Thurston County Chamber Foundation, the county Chamber of Commerce, the local business community, and local and state governments. (www.thurstonchamber.com/Incubator.)

The incubator is typical of many such programs in that it offers clients discounted office space (going up a little bit each year, with a maximum three-year stay); access to office equipment; high-speed Internet; assistance with finances, marketing, and other business practices; and ongoing consulting services. "These services combine to provide significantly lower overhead costs that aids growth and success. Most smaller companies cannot afford to hire this type of support; it would be too demanding on their operating capital."

To get into the program, the first step is a review of a company's business plan by the incubator's staff. Businesses must be locally owned and full-time ventures. The first interview is then held "to determine whether the Incubator can provide useful services to the company." After that, a formal application must be presented to determine "if the company is a good fit for the Incubator's mission of strengthening the local economy through its growth and employment." If accepted, a business is expected to move into the facility. It then gets to take advantage of the services, discounts, networking, and counseling the incubator offers.

Bottom Line: Whether it is through direct investments, free or discounted services, mentoring, networking, or a combination of all of these, business incubators can help any business—with funding and a whole lot more.

CHAPTER 23

Barter

Essential Idea: Swap Products or Services with Like-Minded Businesses and Entrepreneurs

When Norman (name changed) walked into my old law office, I thought I had finally landed the big fish. His construction business grossed more than $1 million a year and he had a lot of legal problems. He was being sued left and right and an employee had embezzled a lot of money. I figured that not only could I help resolve his problems, but I would be in billing heaven for at least the next year.

But while I did work for Norman for a year, I never saw a penny in billable dollars. It turned out that Norman's troubles were so big that he did not have the money, not even close, to pay me for my services. What he proposed instead was a barter arrangement in which he would work on my house and I would provide him with attorney services. I agreed.

I spent a year sorting through and resolving Norman's many legal issues, and he spent a year upgrading my home. He added a custom deck in the backyard, a porch in the front, and he refurbished a bathroom. It turned out to a great deal for him and a great deal for me. Would I have liked the money instead? Of course. But the work he did was top-notch and it increased the value of our home.

Bartering may not be cash, but in the right circumstances, it's just as good.

BARTER BUCKS

Throughout this book I have referred to "in-kind contributions." An in-kind contribution is not the same as cash, but it has cash value. When a lawyer donates his time to a nonprofit, when a doctor volunteers her services to the needy, these are in-kind contributions. While not cash contributions, they do have significant cash value and may be even more valuable.

The same is true for barter. Norman's work on my house had value, significant value, just the same as money has value. So, as you look for direct funding for your business, do not discount the in-kind cash value of barter. Instead of doling out your hard-earned money to another business, you get to save your money. And not only do you save money, but you still get the benefit of the other business's services or products without having to pay for them.

In its simplest form, barter is simply the exchange of your goods or services for another business's goods or services without trading dollars. As such, it turns out that barter is an excellent method to grow your business in a variety of ways *without using cash*. In this sense, it is not unlike a business incubator in that the money saved is the equivalent of money received. Not cash, but not bad.

The International Reciprocal Trade Association estimates that almost a half million businesses barter in the United States every year. The US Department of Commerce estimates that up to 25 percent of the world's trade is now done through barter, and that corporations engage in $20 billion worth of barter every year.

Source: www.bbu.com.

BARTER BENEFITS

For the small business, there are significant reasons to use barter instead of cash to augment normal business. With barter, you can:

Save money. What would it have cost me to hire Norman to add a deck, build a porch, and redo a bathroom? That barter exchange benefited me financially in two ways. First, I was able to save the money I would have spent to have those things done, and second, I was able to use some of the money I saved for other, more pressing expenditures. Bartering your unused time or unsold inventory rather than money saves you money.

Move excess inventory or unused time. Barter allows you to make good use of products or time that may be otherwise wasted. Stores have extra inventory, accountants have unused time, restaurants have empty tables, and so on. Bartering these valuable, albeit unused, assets allows you to get valuable assets in return.

Create new customers. Bartering, when done the right way, exposes new people to your business and helps grow it in a few ways:

1. If you join a barter exchange, members of the exchange become exposed to your business. Bonus: It costs you nothing to gain the exposure.
2. In addition, the people who barter for your goods or services just may become regular, paying clients.
3. Finally: Since word-of-mouth advertising is one of the best marketing tools there is, satisfied barter customers can also send cash-paying customers your way.

Increase your cash reserves. As indicated, and significantly, by bartering for the products and services you need and use most, you can save your capital for other things.

Even out sales. If yours is a seasonal business, barter can be used during slow months to keep things flowing, and can then be used less during your high season. If you have a restaurant that is not sold out, you can barter reservations. If you are a professional, you can barter unbilled time.

Dave's dive shop is very busy in the spring and summer months, but slow in the cooler months. So Dave makes sure to always include a few barter dives during the summer, knowing that (1) he can always get people interested in a barter dive in the summer, and (2) he can redeem the exchange later, when he is less busy, for whatever he needs. Dave has used this to take winter trips with his family, and get work done on his shop.

Tap into the need for some companies to move things that can perish. Many items become worthless if not sold or bartered in a timely fashion, and this can really benefit your business. Unused hotel rooms, rental cars, food, and other travel and entertainment services need to be moved, or lost for good.

Create employee incentives. All sorts of tangible incentives for your employees—travel, restaurants, spas, and so forth—can be had without spending a dime, using barter. Alternatively, you could simply give each employee a certain amount of your barter credits to use as they wish.

From a marketing perspective, there are several additional benefits to barter. For starters, the more money you save by bartering, the more you are able to earmark toward marketing. In addition, companies that have ad space, be it in a magazine, in a newspaper, online, or in radio or TV time, may be active in various barter systems because their goods are also perishable; that is, if those five minutes of ad time are neither sold nor bartered, they are gone forever. This means that you can use barter to obtain some of that media space to grow your business.

Is barter cash? No, but it sure is nice nonetheless.

BRANDS OF BARTER

There are two forms of barter. The oldest method is called "direct" barter. This is where you simply trade your business's items for those of another company. This is what I did with Norman. The key is to have something someone else wants or needs and then to make contact. You may be surprised how many companies may be open to your barter suggestion.

While direct barter is still quite popular, these days a significant amount of barter is done online via "barter exchanges," and it may be easier for you to proceed that way. A barter exchange is a company that brings together many different people and businesses desiring to barter, and then facilitates the transfer of their goods and services. Specifically, a barter exchange acts as a middleman that:

- Keeps track of what you have sold, and bought, within the system.
- Issues "barter bucks" to you when you do something for someone else in the group, which you later use to buy the goods or services from anyone else in the group.

- Sends out monthly statements to all member businesses, detailing purchases made, services rendered, and account balances.

For example, say that Carl the chiropractor charges $100 per session and joins a barter exchange. If Carl does five sessions of treatments for someone in the group, the barter exchange will issue him $500 in barter bucks, or barter credit. He can then use this "money" on any other product or service offered by any other member.

Needless to say, the caveat is that if your business provides a specialized or highly unique service there will not be much need for what you are offering. In that case, this is not the strategy for you. But if what you offer is fairly ubiquitous, then barter can save and make you a lot of money.

> Jill started a graphic design business and one of the first things she did was to join two different barter exchange groups. She meets with about 10 barter clients a year and takes most, but not all, of the jobs offered. Upon completion of the projects, some of these clients stick around and become regular paying customers, others continue to be barter customers, and still others are just one-off deals. Many refer new, cash-paying clients to Jill as well.

THE BARTER TRAIL

If you would like to use barter to increase your business, here are the steps to take:

1. *Decide what sort of barter system works best for you.* Direct or barter exchange? If you already have someone lined up to engage in direct barter with, great. If not, you will need to put out feelers. Once you do find a direct barter partner, it is vital that the two of you agree on an appropriate value for one another's services so that things even out. You want to avoid bartering your products or services for things of lesser value.

2. *If you choose an exchange, do your research.* Use the terms "Barter and Trade Exchanges" in your online search. Different exchanges offer different benefits. Then check out the exchanges you like with the

Better Business Bureau and Yelp, and even consider pulling a Dun & Bradstreet credit report on them. Also, you may want them to be members of the International Reciprocal Trade Association (IRTA.) If you can communicate with current members, that would be very helpful too.

3. *Understand the fees.* In the pre-Internet days, a barter exchange might charge a membership fee of several hundred dollars, a monthly fee of around $20, and a commission on each transaction, split between the buyer and seller, of about 10 percent. Today, most online barter groups charge much less. Joining may be free and transaction fees may be as little as 2 percent. However, also know that fees should not be the sole determining factor. A more expensive group may have a bigger, more diverse membership, thereby offering more products, services, and benefits.

4. *Join and grow.* Join your group, barter, and get involved. The more you put in, the more you will get out.

5. *Do the paperwork.* Even though barter is a cashless exchange, that does not mean that it is not a taxable event. It is (no surprise there!). So be sure to report what you sell as income on your federal tax return, and deduct what you buy as an expense. Expect to receive a 1099 at the end of each tax year from the exchange.

Resources you can use:

- International Reciprocal Trade Association: www.IRTA.com
- Business Barter News: www.barternews.com
- Business Xchange: www.BizX.com
- Itex barter: www.Itex.com
- Barter Card: www.Bartercard.com

Bottom Line: Barter may not be cash in your pocket, but it is the next best thing.

The end.

Appendix: The Business Plan

This sample business plan has been made available to users of *Business Plan Pro*®, business planning software published by Palo Alto Software, Inc. Names, locations and numbers may have been changed, and substantial portions of the original plan text may have been omitted to preserve confidentiality and proprietary information.

You are welcome to use this plan as a starting point to create your own, but you do not have permission to resell, reproduce, publish, distribute or even copy this plan as it exists here.

Requests for reprints, academic use, and other dissemination of this sample plan should be emailed to the marketing department of Palo Alto Software at marketing@paloalto.com. For product information visit their website: www.paloalto.com or call: 1-800-229-7526.

1.0 EXECUTIVE SUMMARY

Emerald Driving Range (Emerald, EDR) is a new enterprise that provides state-of-the-art facilities that accommodate golfers of all levels. A first-class driving range with slots for 50 golfers along with two chipping greens and two putting greens will be available. EDR will focus on providing practice opportunities for golfers of all abilities. There will be a PGA Teaching Pro to give lessons on a daily basis. We will have a concessions area that will provide a variety of drinks and snack foods for golfers who need to take a break.

It is our purpose to set a strategic direction for our future and this is the primary purpose of this business plan. It will address location, finance, and service issues that will be key to the future success of the business. This process is challenging from the standpoint that there are several other driving ranges in the community and we are a start-up enterprise. What we have to offer in facilities is unique to the industry, and we are excited to serve the community.

Our market strategy is based on becoming a viable choice for people looking for a place to practice every aspect of the game of golf. The three target market segments Emerald is focusing on are Children, Adults, and Schools. Golf is becoming increasingly popular with children at younger ages. We will have programs in place to meet the needs of kids wanting to learn the game of golf. Our facility will also appeal to adults of all levels who want a quality place to practice or take lessons. Emerald will also build relationships with local schools and universities to hold classes at the range, and to use it as a practice facility for their golf teams. The marketing objective is to actively support continued growth and profitability through effective implementation of the strategy.

1.1 Mission

Emerald Driving Range is dedicated to providing a practice facility that is committed to serving golfers, both advanced and novice. It is our purpose to manage a facility that will help golfers of all levels develop their game. Emerald will strive to make each customer feel that they are important to our business and will give each customer value for their dollar. Emerald realizes that each employee is a valuable asset to the company and will encourage a team atmosphere and will treat each employee with respect.

1.2 Objectives

1. Sales improving steadily through year three.
2. Remarkably high Gross Margin.
3. Net income/sales positively modest each year.

Chart: Highlights

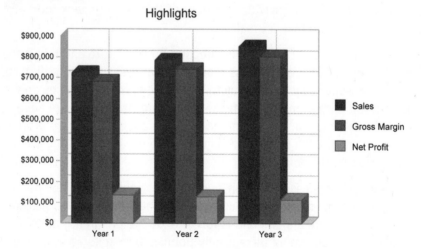

1.3 Keys to Success

1. Provide excellent customer service with a proactive energetic staff.

2. Provide a top notch facility that allows customers to work on every aspect of the game.

3. Provide quality instruction from beginner to expert.

2.0 COMPANY SUMMARY

Emerald Driving Range is a new enterprise that provides state-of-the-art facilities that will accommodate golfers of all levels. There will be an on-site PGA Teaching Pro giving lessons on a daily basis. Emerald will focus on providing practice opportunities to the recreational golfer as well as the serious competitive golfer. Arrangements will be made with local schools and universities to use the facility for their golf teams' practices and golf classes. A first-class driving range is available with slots that accommodate 50 golfers at a time. Chipping greens with sand traps as well as two putting greens will be in place.

2.1 Start-up Summary

Total start-up expense (including development of facility) are shown below. Long-term assets include a ball retrieving machine as well as other maintenance equipment. Other expenses include balls, clubs, towels, and misc. accessories. We will have a concessions area that will provide a variety of drinks and snack foods for golfers who need to take a break. The details are included in the following table.

Table: Start-up

Start-up	
Requirements	
Start-up Expenses	
Legal	$ 1,000
Stationery etc.	$ 500
Brochures	$ 1,500
Consultants	$ 3,000
Insurance	$ 1,000
Rent	$ 2,000
	(*Continued*)

Research and Development	$ 40,000
Expensed Equipment	$ 10,000
Concessions	$ 4,000
Total Start-up Expenses	$ 63,000
Start-up Assets	
Cash Required	$ 40,000
Other Current Assets	$ 0
Long-term Assets	$ 27,000
Total Assets	$ 67,000
Total Requirements	**$130,000**

Table: Start-up Funding

Start-up Funding	
Start-up Expenses to Fund	$ 63,000
Start-up Assets to Fund	$ 67,000
Total Funding Required	$130,000
Assets	
Non-cash Assets from Start-up	$ 27,000
Cash Requirements from Start-up	$ 40,000
Additional Cash Raised	$ 0
Cash Balance on Starting Date	$ 40,000
Total Assets	$ 67,000
Liabilities and Capital	
Liabilities	
Current Borrowing	$ 0
Long-term Liabilities	$ 0
Accounts Payable (Outstanding Bills)	$ 0
Other Current Liabilities (interest-free)	$ 0
Total Liabilities	$ 0
	(Continued)

Capital

Planned Investment	
Stan Walker	$ 20,000
Fred Fast	$ 20,000
Jim Spade	$ 20,000
Additional Investment Requirement	$ 70,000
Total Planned Investment	$130,000
Loss at Start-up (Start-up Expenses)	($ 63,000)
Total Capital	$ 67,000
Total Capital and Liabilities	$ 67,000
Total Funding	$130,000

Chart: Start-up

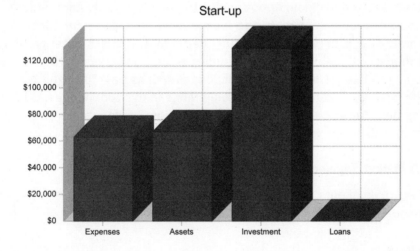

2.2 Company Ownership

Emerald Driving Range will be created as a partnership with Stan Walker owning $33\frac{1}{2}$%, Fred Fast $33\frac{1}{2}$%, and Jim Spade $33\frac{1}{2}$%. Stan Walker will act as president, with Fred Fast and Jim Spade on the management team, handling marketing/advertising and concessions/vendors respectively.

3.0 SERVICES

Emerald Driving Range provides golfers with a practice facility that will focus on all aspects of the game. We welcome golfers of all abilities, and have an on-site professional to give instruction to those who wish to do so. We will offer a variety of beverages and snack foods for our patrons to enjoy while they take a break from practicing.

4.0 MARKET ANALYSIS SUMMARY

Emerald Driving Range will be focusing on golfers at all levels and all ages who want a good quality practice facility.

Our target groups include children (ages 6-17), and we are developing a program for them to participate in. Golf is becoming more and more popular and as kids are beginning to participate at younger ages we would like to give them opportunities to learn the game. Another target group is adults, both male and female, who have an interest in either learning the game of golf, or getting better at it. The last target group is comprised of high schools, local colleges, and universities who want a facility to have classes and instruction, as well as train their golf teams. The need for a state-of-the-art driving range in this community has been apparent for many years and Emerald Driving Range intends to satisfy that need.

4.1 Market Segmentation

The profile of our customers consists of the following Psychographic and Demographic factors.

Adults
- 70% male.
- Age range of 18 years to 65.
- Average annual household income of $70,000.
- Professional/white collar worker.
- Plays for business as well as pleasure.

Children

- Age 7 to 17.
- Parents play golf.
- Play other sports in addition to golf.

Schools

- School sizes range between 500 to 2,000 students for high schools in the area.
- Community colleges and university have approximately 40,000 students combined.
- 10% of the local schools are private institutions.
- 40% of high schools and colleges/universities have an active golf team.

Table: Market Analysis

Market Analysis

Potential Customers	Growth	Year 1	Year 2	Year 3	Year 4	Year 5	CAGR
Adults	10%	50,000	55,000	60,500	66,550	73,205	10.00%
Children	10%	60,000	66,000	72,600	79,860	87,846	10.00%
Schools	10%	5,000	5,500	6,050	6,655	7,321	10.00%
Total	10.00%	115,000	126,500	139,150	153,065	168,372	10.00%

Chart: Market Analysis (Pie)

Market Analysis (Pie)

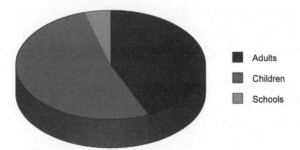

- Adults
- Children
- Schools

4.2 Target Market Segment Strategy

Our market strategy is based on becoming a viable choice for people looking for a place to practice every aspect of the game of golf. We will have a resident professional with an assistant to assist those customers who wish to have lessons. The target markets are separated into three segments; "Children," "Adults," and "Schools".

Children – Age range of 9 to 17 years of age. Most of the parents of these children also play golf. In addition to golf many of this group plays other sports. Most of these kids also come from middle- to upper-class families.

Adults – This group has an age range of 18 to 59 years of age. 70% of this group are males (professional/white collar worker) with an annual household income in excess of $70,000 dollars. It is common for this group to play for business as well as pleasure. Many companies also use golf as a company event for its employees.

Schools – Many local high schools in the area have golf teams that need local practice facilities. With a university and community college in the area the need for convenient practice facilities exists. Working with these institutions to provide facilities to hold classes and practice will fill this need. Local high schools typically have 500 to 2,000 students. With ten schools in the area we are looking at approximately 15,000 students. Private schools only make up about 10% of the schools in the area. The university and community college have combined enrollments of approximately 40,000 students.

4.3 Service Business Analysis

The Driving Range business entails providing a facility that allows for practice in every aspect of the game. Driving, chipping, and putting.

4.3.1 Competition and Buying Patterns

With the increased popularity of golf and the limited number of practice facilities in the area, people will welcome another choice.

Main competitors:

> **Fiddler's Green** – Par 3 18-hole golf course with a driving range and clubhouse selling golf equipment. On-site professional is available to give lessons. Driving range is small but well equipped. Location is not convenient for many people as it is out of town a few miles.
>
> **Riveridge** – Regulation 18-hole course with a large driving range and pro shop. Located in town, it is convenient to get to and is a well run facility.
>
> **Laurelwood** – A large nine-hole municipal course with a small driving range and pro shop. Convenient in town location but the driving range is very small and outdated.

All of the driving ranges in the area also have golf courses as part of the facility. The quality of the golf course is usually one of the main draws for people to come and practice. Location also plays a big part in how many consumers choose their practice facility. Driving ranges with an on-site professional draw people who are looking for instruction.

5.0 STRATEGY AND IMPLEMENTATION SUMMARY

The primary sales and marketing strategy includes these factors:

- A quality practice facility that allows a golfer to work on every part of his or her game.
- Availability of quality instruction by a certified PGA Teaching Professional.
- Open facility to high schools, colleges and universities to hold classes and team practice sessions.

5.1 Competitive Edge

Emerald Driving Range believes its competitive edge lies with two main differentiators.

1. We do not have to deal with the day-to-day operations of running a golf course, so we can give more attention to our customers, as well as give more focus to the facility itself.
2. Our facility is set up to accommodate more golfers at a time than most of our competitors. Our customer service will be top notch and we will have a good variety of beverages and snack foods for customers.

5.2 Marketing Strategy

Our marketing strategy is based on becoming the preferred choice for golfers of all ages who are looking for a practice facility that focuses on all phases of the game. Our marketing strategy is based on superior service in the following areas:

- Quality facilities.
- Quality instruction.
- Customer service.

Our marketing strategy will create interest and appeal from our target market for what we offer our customers. Once they come to our facility we have no doubt that they will not only come back, but will bring their friends as well.

5.3 Sales Strategy

The primary sales and marketing strategy includes these factors:

- A satisfying practice experience that provides excellent facilities and top notch customer service.
- An on-site professional to give lessons and individual instruction.
- Excellent location that is convenient to get to.

5.3.1 Sales Forecast

The Sales Forecast is broken down into three main revenue streams: Driving Range & Practice Facilities, Concessions, and Professional Lessons. The Sales Forecast for the upcoming year is based on a modest 5% growth rate for each of these revenue streams. In spite of any economic unpredictability in the future, we expect to have at least a 5% growth increase in the following two years.

Table: Sales Forecast

Sales Forecast

	Year 1	Year 2	Year 3
Sales			
Driving Range & Practice Facilities	$491,000	$540,100	$594,110
Concessions	$108,223	$113,634	$119,316
Professional Lessons	$126,000	$132,300	$138,915
Total Sales	$725,223	$786,034	$852,341
Direct Cost of Sales	Year 1	Year 2	Year 3
Driving Range & Practice Facilities	$ 0	$ 0	$ 0
Concessions	$ 43,289	$ 45,454	$ 47,726
Professional Lessons	$ 0	$ 0	$ 0
Subtotal Direct Cost of Sales	$ 43,289	$ 45,454	$ 47,726

Chart: Sales Monthly

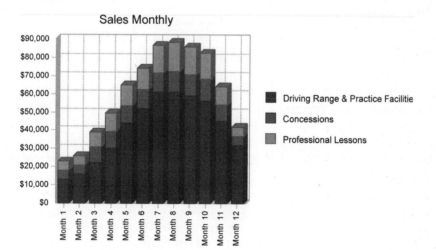

Chart: Sales by Year

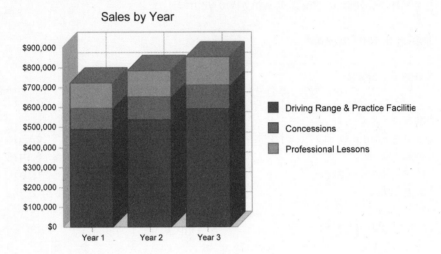

Sales by Year

Legend:
- Driving Range & Practice Facilitie
- Concessions
- Professional Lessons

5.4 Milestones

The Milestones table outlines key activities that will be critical to our success in the coming year.

Table: Milestones

Milestones

Milestone	Start Date	End Date	Budget	Manager	Department
Business Plan	1/1/2003	1/15/2003	$ 500	Stan	Management
Marketing & Advertising	2/20/2003	6/10/2003	$ 1,500	Fred	Management
Lesson Schedule	8/21/2003	11/25/2003	$ 500	Joe	Golf Pro
Sourcing Food Vendors	5/20/2003	6/8/2003	$ 1,000	Jim	Management
Web Plan	3/15/2003	4/18/2003	$ 500	Fred	Management
Accounting Plan	5/1/2003	5/30/2003	$ 500	Stan	Management
Maintenance Plan	7/14/2003	8/28/2003	$ 500	Jerry	Maintenance
Totals			$5,000		

Chart: Milestones

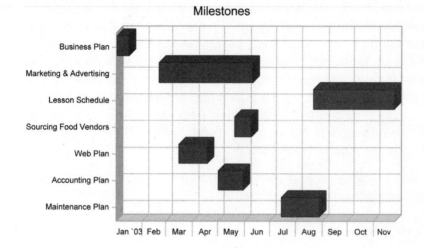

6.0 MANAGEMENT SUMMARY

Stan Walker oversees all of the operations at Emerald Driving Range. Fred has the responsibility for the marketing and advertising of the business along with the creation and implementation of the Web page. Jim is responsible for overseeing the concessions which includes all ordering and dealing with vendors.

Stan also handles the accounting for the driving range. Stan Walker has 15 years experience working as an active manager for the prestigious Mckenzie Golf Club. Stan managed the day-to-day operations including the driving range. Golf instruction has been a passion of Stan's and through years of planning the idea of Emerald Driving Range was seen to fruition. Fred and Jim also have worked in the industry for the last 20 years, each in management capacities. Jim managed the Spring Creek driving range and has been a personal friend of Stan's for many years. Fred has spent the last 10 years in the advertising business working with a golf magazine.

6.1 Personnel Plan

The personnel plan consists of Stan Walker taking a salary of $48,000 per year. Fred Fast and Jim Spade will each draw $36,000 out of the business for their contributions. Fred and Jim are not working at the site full time but will share a percentage of the profits at the end of the year. There will be one full-time greenskeeper making $2,500 per month, four full-time employees making $2,000 per month, and four part-time employees working 16 hours per week each, making $10.00 per hour. Our resident golf pro Joe Bain will draw a salary of $4,000 per month and Joe's assistant Todd Smith will work part-time at $1,500 per month.

Salary increases in year 2005 and 2006 will be set conservatively at 5% to mirror projected sales increases.

Table: Personnel

Personnel Plan

	Year 1	Year 2	Year 3
Stan Walker	$ 48,000	$ 50,400	$ 52,920
Part-time Employees	$ 36,000	$ 47,250	$ 59,535
Full-time Employees	$126,000	$165,375	$208,373
Fred Fast	$ 36,000	$ 37,800	$ 39,690
Golf Pros	$ 66,000	$ 69,300	$ 72,765
Jim Spade	$ 36,000	$ 37,800	$ 39,690
Total People	14	16	18
Total Payroll	$348,000	$407,925	$472,973

7.0 FINANCIAL PLAN

The financial plan contains these essential factors:

- A growth rate in sales of 5% for the year 2005, to $786,000 in total revenues.

- An average sales per business day (340 days per year) in excess of $2,300.

Difficulties and Risks:

- Slow sales resulting in less-than projected cash flow.
- A parallel entry into the market by another competitor.
- Unexpected cost increases compared with the forecasted sales.

7.1 Important Assumptions

The following assumptions will determine the potential for future success.

- A healthy economy that supports a moderate level of growth in our market.
- The ability to maintain at least a 5% growth each year.
- Keeping operating costs low, particularly in the area of personnel and ongoing monthly expenses.

Table: General Assumptions

General Assumptions

	Year 1	Year 2	Year 3
Plan Month	1	2	3
Current Interest Rate	8.00%	8.00%	8.00%
Long-term Interest Rate	7.50%	7.50%	7.50%
Tax Rate	28.17%	28.00%	28.17%
Other	0	0	0

7.2 Break-even Analysis

The following chart and table summarize our break-even analysis. We don't really expect to reach break-even until a few months into the business operation. We will be charging $4.00 for a bucket of balls and we speculate that if for every two buckets of balls purchased we sell one drink at a cost of $2.00 we will have an average cost per unit of 25%.

Table: Break-even Analysis

Break-even Analysis	
Monthly Revenue Break-even	$43,860
Assumptions: Average Percent Variable Cost	6%
Estimated Monthly Fixed Cost	**$41,242**

Chart: Break-even Analysis

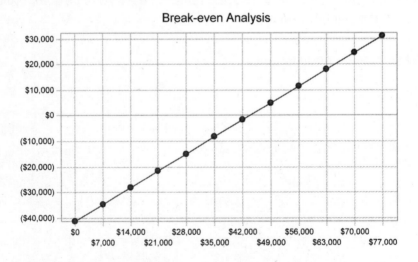

Break-even Analysis

7.3 Projected Profit and Loss

The following represents the projected profit and loss for Emerald Driving Range based on sales and expense projections for 2004 and beyond.

Chart: Profit Monthly

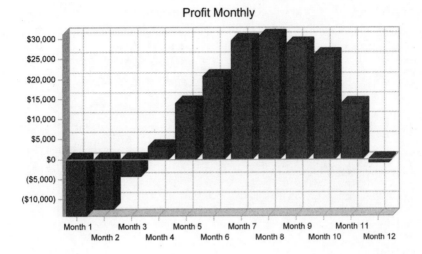

Chart: Profit Yearly

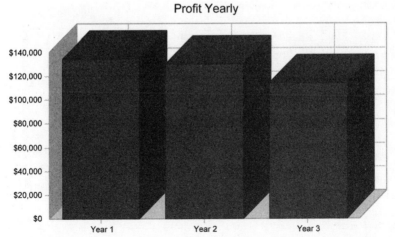

Chart: Gross Margin Monthly

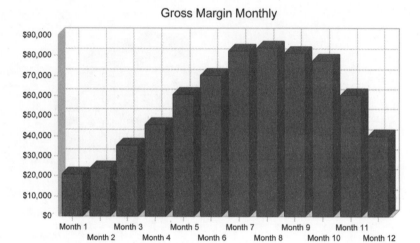

Chart: Gross Margin Yearly

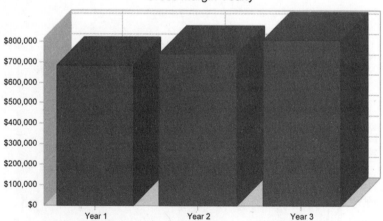

Table: Profit and Loss

Pro Forma Profit and Loss

	Year 1	Year 2	Year 3
Sales	$725,223	$786,034	$852,341
Direct Cost of Sales	$ 43,289	$ 45,454	$ 47,726
Other Costs of Sales	$ 0	$ 0	$ 0
Total Cost of Sales	$ 43,289	$ 45,454	$ 47,726
Gross Margin	$681,934	$740,581	$804,615
Gross Margin %	94.03%	94.22%	94.40%
Expenses			
Payroll	$348,000	$407,925	$472,973
Sales and Marketing and Other Expenses	$ 12,000	$ 17,000	$ 27,000
Depreciation	$ 1,704	$ 1,714	$ 1,714
Rent	$ 48,000	$ 36,000	$ 36,000
Utilities	$ 12,000	$ 13,000	$ 13,000
Insurance	$ 12,000	$ 13,000	$ 13,000
Payroll Taxes	$ 52,200	$ 61,189	$ 70,946
Other	$ 9,000	$ 10,000	$ 11,000
Total Operating Expenses	$494,904	$559,828	$645,633
Profit Before Interest and Taxes	$187,030	$180,753	$158,982
EBITDA	$188,734	$182,467	$160,696
Interest Expense	$ 0	$ 0	$ 0
Taxes Incurred	$ 51,964	$ 50,611	$ 44,780
Net Profit	$135,066	$130,142	$114,202
Net Profit/Sales	18.62%	16.56%	13.40%

7.4 Projected Cash Flow

The cash flow projections are outlined below. Again, these projections are based on our basic assumptions with revenue generation factors carrying the most significant weight regarding the outcome.

Chart: Cash

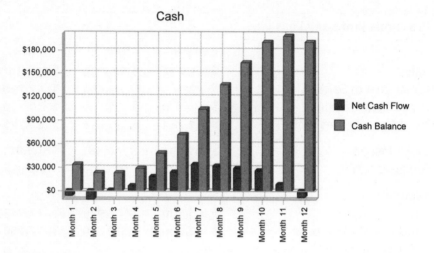

Table: Cash Flow

Pro Forma Cash Flow

	Year 1	Year 2	Year 3
Cash Received			
Cash from Operations			
Cash Sales	$725,223	$786,034	$852,341
Cash from Receivables	$ 0	$ 0	$ 0
Subtotal Cash from Operations	$725,223	$786,034	$852,341
Additional Cash Received			
Sales Tax, VAT, HST/GST Received	$ 0	$ 0	$ 0
New Current Borrowing	$ 0	$ 0	$ 0
New Other Liabilities (interest-free)	$ 0	$ 0	$ 0
New Long-term Liabilities	$ 0	$ 0	$ 0
Sales of Other Current Assets	$ 0	$ 0	$ 0
Sales of Long-term Assets	$ 0	$ 0	$ 0
New Investment Received	$ 0	$ 0	$ 0
Subtotal Cash Received	$725,223	$786,034	$852,341

(Continued)

Expenditures	Year 1	Year 2	Year 3
Expenditures from Operations			
Cash Spending	$348,000	$407,925	$472,973
Bill Payments	$227,159	$239,307	$262,039
Subtotal Spent on Operations	$575,159	$647,232	$735,012
Additional Cash Spent			
Sales Tax, VAT, HST/GST Paid Out	$ 0	$ 0	$ 0
Principal Repayment of Current Borrowing	$ 0	$ 0	$ 0
Other Liabilities Principal Repayment	$ 0	$ 0	$ 0
Long-term Liabilities Principal Repayment	$ 0	$ 0	$ 0
Purchase Other Current Assets	$ 0	$ 0	$ 0
Purchase Long-term Assets	$ 0	$ 0	$ 0
Dividends	$ 0	$ 40,000	$ 40,000
Subtotal Cash Spent	$575,159	$687,232	$775,012
Net Cash Flow	$150,064	$ 98,802	$ 77,329
Cash Balance	$190,064	$288,866	$366,196

7.5 Projected Balance Sheet

Emerald Driving Range's balance sheet is outlined below.

Table: Balance Sheet

Pro Forma Balance Sheet

	Year 1	Year 2	Year 3
Assets			
Current Assets			
Cash	$190,064	$288,866	$366,196
Accounts Receivable	$ 0	$ 0	$ 0
Other Current Assets	$ 0	$ 0	$ 0
Total Current Assets	$190,064	$288,866	$366,196

(Continued)

Long-term Assets			
Long-term Assets	$ 27,000	$ 27,000	$ 27,000
Accumulated Depreciation	$ 1,704	$ 3,418	$ 5,132
Total Long-term Assets	$ 25,296	$ 23,582	$ 21,868
Total Assets	$ 215,360	$ 312,448	$388,064

Liabilities and Capital	Year 1	Year 2	Year 3
Current Liabilities			
Accounts Payable	$ 13,294	$ 20,240	$ 21,654
Current Borrowing	$ 0	$ 0	$ 0
Other Current Liabilities	$ 0	$ 0	$ 0
Subtotal Current Liabilities	$ 13,294	$ 20,240	$ 21,654
Long-term Liabilities	$ 0	$ 0	$ 0
Total Liabilities	$ 13,294	$ 20,240	$ 21,654
Paid-in Capital	$ 130,000	$ 130,000	$ 130,000
Retained Earnings	($ 63,000)	$ 32,066	$ 122,208
Earnings	$ 135,066	$ 130,142	$ 114,202
Total Capital	$ 202,066	$ 292,208	$ 366,410
Total Liabilities and Capital	$ 215,360	$ 312,448	$388,064
Net Worth	$202,066	$292,208	$ 366,410

7.6 Business Ratios

Business Ratios for the years of this plan are shown below. Industry profile ratios based on the Standard Industrial Classification (SIC) code 7999-0202 Driving Ranges are shown for comparison. The following will enable us to keep on track. If we fail in any of these areas, we will need to re-evaluate our business model.

- Gross margins at or above 80%.
- Month-to-month annual comparisons indicate an increase of 5% or greater.
- Do not depend on a credit line to meet cash requirements.

Table: Ratios

Ratio Analysis

	Year 1	Year 2	Year 3	Industry Profile
Sales Growth	n.a.	8.39%	8.44%	5.73%
Percent of Total Assets				
Accounts Receivable	0.00%	0.00%	0.00%	7.08%
Other Current Assets	0.00%	0.00%	0.00%	33.26%
Total Current Assets	88.25%	92.45%	94.36%	43.21%
Long-term Assets	11.75%	7.55%	5.64%	56.79%
Total Assets	100.00%	100.00%	100.00%	100.00%
Current Liabilities	6.17%	6.48%	5.58%	21.91%
Long-term Liabilities	0.00%	0.00%	0.00%	28.81%
Total Liabilities	6.17%	6.48%	5.58%	50.72%
Net Worth	93.83%	93.52%	94.42%	49.28%
Percent of Sales				
Sales	100.00%	100.00%	100.00%	100.00%
Gross Margin	94.03%	94.22%	94.40%	100.00%
Selling, General & Administrative Expenses	75.46%	77.66%	80.97%	76.43%
Advertising Expenses	0.00%	0.00%	0.00%	2.77%
Profit Before Interest and Taxes	25.79%	23.00%	18.65%	1.89%
Main Ratios				
Current	14.30	14.27	16.91	1.18
Quick	14.30	14.27	16.91	0.80
Total Debt to Total Assets	6.17%	6.48%	5.58%	61.12%
Pre-tax Return on Net Worth	92.56%	61.86%	43.39%	1.76%
Pre-tax Return on Assets	86.85%	57.85%	40.97%	4.52%

(*Continued*)

Additional Ratios	Year 1	Year 2	Year 3	Industry Profile
Net Profit Margin	18.62%	16.56%	13.40%	n.a.
Return on Equity	66.84%	44.54%	31.17%	n.a.
Activity Ratios				
Accounts Receivable Turnover	0.00	0.00	0.00	n.a.
Collection Days	0	0	0	n.a.
Accounts Payable Turnover	18.09	12.17	12.17	n.a.
Payment Days	27	25	29	n.a.
Total Asset Turnover	3.37	2.52	2.20	n.a.
Debt Ratios				
Debt to Net Worth	0.07	0.07	0.06	n.a.
Current Liab. to Liab.	1.00	1.00	1.00	n.a.
Liquidity Ratios				
Net Working Capital	$176,770	$268,626	$344,542	n.a.
Interest Coverage	0.00	0.00	0.00	n.a.
Additional Ratios				
Assets to Sales	0.30	0.40	0.46	n.a.
Current Debt/ Total Assets	6%	6%	6%	n.a.
Acid Test	14.30	14.27	16.91	n.a.
Sales/Net Worth	3.59	2.69	2.33	n.a.
Dividend Payout	0.00	0.31	0.35	n.a.

Table: Sales Forecast

Sales Forecast

		Month 1	Month 2	Month 3	Month 4	Month 5	Month 6	Month 7	Month 8	Month 9	Month 10	Month 11	Month 12
Sales													
Driving Range & Practice Facilities	0%	$13,000	$16,000	$22,000	$30,000	$44,000	$52,000	$61,000	$61,000	$59,000	$56,000	$45,000	$32,000
Concessions	0%	$ 5,000	$ 5,000	$ 8,820	$ 9,261	$ 9,724	$ 10,210	$ 10,721	$ 11,257	$ 11,820	$ 12,411	$ 9,000	$ 5,000
Professional Lessons	0%	$ 5,000	$ 5,000	$ 8,000	$ 10,000	$ 11,000	$ 12,000	$ 15,000	$ 16,000	$ 15,000	$ 14,000	$ 10,000	$ 5,000
Total Sales		$23,000	$26,000	$38,820	$49,261	$64,724	$74,210	$86,721	$88,257	$85,820	$82,411	$64,000	$42,000
		Month 1	Month 2	Month 3	Month 4	Month 5	Month 6	Month 7	Month 8	Month 9	Month 10	Month 11	Month 12
Direct Cost of Sales													
Driving Range & Practice Facilities		$ 0	$ 0	$ 0	$ 0	$ 0	$ 0	$ 0	$ 0	$ 0	$ 0	$ 0	$ 0
Concessions		$ 2,000	$ 2,000	$ 3,528	$ 3,704	$ 3,890	$ 4,084	$ 4,288	$ 4,503	$ 4,728	$ 4,964	$ 3,600	$ 2,000
Professional Lessons		$ 0	$ 0	$ 0	$ 0	$ 0	$ 0	$ 0	$ 0	$ 0	$ 0	$ 0	$ 0
Subtotal Direct Cost of Sales		$ 2,000	$ 2,000	$ 3,528	$ 3,704	$ 3,890	$ 4,084	$ 4,288	$ 4,503	$ 4,728	$ 4,964	$ 3,600	$ 2,000

Table: Personnel

Personnel Plan

		Month 1	Month 2	Month 3	Month 4	Month 5	Month 6	Month 7	Month 8	Month 9	Month 10	Month 11	Month 12
Stan Walker	0%	$ 4,000	$ 4,000	$ 4,000	$ 4,000	$ 4,000	$ 4,000	$ 4,000	$ 4,000	$ 4,000	$ 4,000	$ 4,000	$ 4,000
Part-time Employees	0%	$ 3,000	$ 3,000	$ 3,000	$ 3,000	$ 3,000	$ 3,000	$ 3,000	$ 3,000	$ 3,000	$ 3,000	$ 3,000	$ 3,000
Full-time Employees	0%	$10,500	$10,500	$10,500	$10,500	$10,500	$10,500	$10,500	$10,500	$10,500	$10,500	$10,500	$10,500
Fred Fast	0%	$ 3,000	$ 3,000	$ 3,000	$ 3,000	$ 3,000	$ 3,000	$ 3,000	$ 3,000	$ 3,000	$ 3,000	$ 3,000	$ 3,000
Golf Pros	0%	$ 5,500	$ 5,500	$ 5,500	$ 5,500	$ 5,500	$ 5,500	$ 5,500	$ 5,500	$ 5,500	$ 5,500	$ 5,500	$ 5,500
Jim Spade	0%	$ 3,000	$ 3,000	$ 3,000	$ 3,000	$ 3,000	$ 3,000	$ 3,000	$ 3,000	$ 3,000	$ 3,000	$ 3,000	$ 3,000
Total People		14	14	14	14	14	14	14	14	14	14	14	14
Total Payroll		$29,000	$29,000	$29,000	$29,000	$29,000	$29,000	$29,000	$29,000	$29,000	$29,000	$29,000	$29,000

Table: General Assumptions

General Assumptions

	Month 1	Month 2	Month 3	Month 4	Month 5	Month 6	Month 7	Month 8	Month 9	Month 10	Month 11	Month 12
Plan Month	1	2	3	4	5	6	7	8	9	10	11	12
Current Interest Rate	8.00%	8.00%	8.00%	8.00%	8.00%	8.00%	8.00%	8.00%	8.00%	8.00%	8.00%	8.00%
Long-term Interest Rate	7.50%	7.50%	7.50%	7.50%	7.50%	7.50%	7.50%	7.50%	7.50%	7.50%	7.50%	7.50%
Tax Rate	30.00%	28.00%	28.00%	28.00%	28.00%	28.00%	28.00%	28.00%	28.00%	28.00%	28.00%	28.00%
Other	0	0	0	0	0	0	0	0	0	0	0	0

Table: Profit and Loss

Pro Forma Profit and Loss

	Month 1	Month 2	Month 3	Month 4	Month 5	Month 6	Month 7	Month 8	Month 9	Month 10	Month 11	Month 12
Sales	$ 23,000	$ 26,000	$38,820	$49,261	$64,724	$74,210	$86,721	$88,257	$85,820	$ 82,411	$64,000	$42,000
Direct Cost of Sales	$ 2,000	$ 2,000	$ 3,528	$ 3,704	$ 3,890	$ 4,084	$ 4,288	$ 4,503	$ 4,728	$ 4,964	$ 3,600	$ 2,000
Other Costs of Sales	$ 0	$ 0	$ 0	$ 0	$ 0	$ 0	$ 0	$ 0	$ 0	$ 0	$ 0	$ 0
Total Cost of Sales	$ 2,000	$ 2,000	$ 3,528	$ 3,704	$ 3,890	$ 4,084	$ 4,288	$ 4,503	$ 4,728	$ 4,964	$ 3,600	$ 2,000
Gross Margin	$ 21,000	$ 24,000	$35,292	$45,557	$60,834	$70,126	$82,432	$83,754	$81,092	$77,446	$60,400	$40,000
Gross Margin %	91.30%	92.31%	90.91%	92.48%	93.99%	94.50%	95.06%	94.90%	94.49%	93.98%	94.38%	95.24%
Expenses												
Payroll	$ 29,000	$ 29,000	$29,000	$29,000	$29,000	$29,000	$29,000	$29,000	$29,000	$29,000	$29,000	$29,000
Sales and Marketing and Other Expenses	$ 1,000	$ 1,000	$ 1,000	$ 1,000	$ 1,000	$ 1,000	$ 1,000	$ 1,000	$ 1,000	$ 1,000	$ 1,000	$ 1,000
Depreciation	$ 142	$ 142	$ 142	$ 142	$ 142	$ 142	$ 142	$ 142	$ 142	$ 142	$ 142	$ 142
Rent	$ 4,000	$ 4,000	$ 4,000	$ 4,000	$ 4,000	$ 4,000	$ 4,000	$ 4,000	$ 4,000	$ 4,000	$ 4,000	$ 4,000
Utilities	$ 1,000	$ 1,000	$ 1,000	$ 1,000	$ 1,000	$ 1,000	$ 1,000	$ 1,000	$ 1,000	$ 1,000	$ 1,000	$ 1,000
Insurance	$ 1,000	$ 1,000	$ 1,000	$ 1,000	$ 1,000	$ 1,000	$ 1,000	$ 1,000	$ 1,000	$ 1,000	$ 1,000	$ 1,000
Payroll Taxes 15%	$ 4,350	$ 4,350	$ 4,350	$ 4,350	$ 4,350	$ 4,350	$ 4,350	$ 4,350	$ 4,350	$ 4,350	$ 4,350	$ 4,350
Other	$ 750	$ 750	$ 750	$ 750	$ 750	$ 750	$ 750	$ 750	$ 750	$ 750	$ 750	$ 750
Total Operating Expenses	$ 41,242	$ 41,242	$41,242	$41,242	$41,242	$41,242	$41,242	$41,242	$41,242	$41,242	$41,242	$41,242
Profit Before Interest and Taxes	($ 20,242)	($ 17,242)	($ 5,950)	$ 4,315	$19,592	$28,884	$41,190	$42,512	$39,850	$36,204	$19,158	($ 1,242)
EBITDA	($ 20,100)	($ 17,100)	($ 5,808)	$ 4,457	$19,734	$29,026	$41,332	$42,654	$39,992	$36,346	$19,300	($ 1,100)
Interest Expense	$ 0	$ 0	$ 0	$ 0	$ 0	$ 0	$ 0	$ 0	$ 0	$ 0	$ 0	$ 0
Taxes Incurred	($ 6,073)	($ 4,828)	($ 1,666)	$ 1,208	$ 5,486	$ 8,088	$11,533	$11,903	$11,158	$ 10,137	$ 5,364	($ 348)
Net Profit	($ 14,169)	($ 12,414)	($ 4,284)	$ 3,107	$14,107	$20,797	$29,657	$30,609	$28,692	$26,067	$13,794	($ 894)
Net Profit/Sales	−61.61%	−47.75%	−11.04%	6.31%	21.79%	28.02%	34.20%	34.68%	33.43%	31.63%	21.55%	−2.13%

Table: Cash Flow

Pro Forma Cash Flow

		Month 1	Month 2	Month 3	Month 4	Month 5	Month 6	Month 7	Month 8	Month 9	Month 10	Month 11	Month 12
Cash Received													
Cash from Operations													
Cash Sales		$23,000	$26,000	$38,820	$49,261	$64,724	$74,210	$86,721	$88,257	$85,820	$82,411	$64,000	$42,000
Cash from Receivables		$ 0	$ 0	$ 0	$ 0	$ 0	$ 0	$ 0	$ 0	$ 0	$ 0	$ 0	$ 0
Subtotal Cash from Operations		$23,000	$26,000	$38,820	$49,261	$64,724	$74,210	$86,721	$88,257	$85,820	$82,411	$64,000	$42,000
Additional Cash Received													
Sales Tax, VAT, HST/ GST Received	0.00%	$ 0	$ 0	$ 0	$ 0	$ 0	$ 0	$ 0	$ 0	$ 0	$ 0	$ 0	$ 0
New Current Borrowing		$ 0	$ 0	$ 0	$ 0	$ 0	$ 0	$ 0	$ 0	$ 0	$ 0	$ 0	$ 0
New Other Liabilities (interest-free)		$ 0	$ 0	$ 0	$ 0	$ 0	$ 0	$ 0	$ 0	$ 0	$ 0	$ 0	$ 0
New Long-term Liabilities		$ 0	$ 0	$ 0	$ 0	$ 0	$ 0	$ 0	$ 0	$ 0	$ 0	$ 0	$ 0
Sales of Other Current Assets		$ 0	$ 0	$ 0	$ 0	$ 0	$ 0	$ 0	$ 0	$ 0	$ 0	$ 0	$ 0
Sales of Long-term Assets		$ 0	$ 0	$ 0	$ 0	$ 0	$ 0	$ 0	$ 0	$ 0	$ 0	$ 0	$ 0
New Investment Received		$ 0	$ 0	$ 0	$ 0	$ 0	$ 0	$ 0	$ 0	$ 0	$ 0	$ 0	$ 0
Subtotal Cash Received		$23,000	$26,000	$38,820	$49,261	$64,724	$74,210	$86,721	$88,257	$85,820	$82,411	$64,000	$42,000

(Continued)

Expenditures	Month 1	Month 2	Month 3	Month 4	Month 5	Month 6	Month 7	Month 8	Month 9	Month 10	Month 11	Month 12
Expenditures from Operations												
Cash Spending	$29,000	$29,000	$29,000	$29,000	$29,000	$29,000	$29,000	$29,000	$29,000	$29,000	$29,000	$29,000
Bill Payments	$ 268	$ 8,069	$ 9,429	$14,064	$ 17,161	$ 21,569	$ 24,393	$ 27,941	$ 28,489	$ 27,960	$ 26,997	$ 20,821
Subtotal Spent on Operations	$29,268	$37,069	$38,429	$43,064	$46,161	$50,569	$ 53,393	$ 56,941	$ 57,489	$ 56,960	$ 55,997	$ 49,821
Additional Cash Spent												
Sales Tax, VAT, HST/GST Paid Out	$ 0	$ 0	$ 0	$ 0	$ 0	$ 0	$ 0	$ 0	$ 0	$ 0	$ 0	$ 0
Principal Repayment of Current Borrowing	$ 0	$ 0	$ 0	$ 0	$ 0	$ 0	$ 0	$ 0	$ 0	$ 0	$ 0	$ 0
Other Liabilities Principal Repayment	$ 0	$ 0	$ 0	$ 0	$ 0	$ 0	$ 0	$ 0	$ 0	$ 0	$ 0	$ 0
Long-term Liabilities Principal Repayment	$ 0	$ 0	$ 0	$ 0	$ 0	$ 0	$ 0	$ 0	$ 0	$ 0	$ 0	$ 0
Purchase Other Current Assets	$ 0	$ 0	$ 0	$ 0	$ 0	$ 0	$ 0	$ 0	$ 0	$ 0	$ 0	$ 0
Purchase Long-term Assets	$ 0	$ 0	$ 0	$ 0	$ 0	$ 0	$ 0	$ 0	$ 0	$ 0	$ 0	$ 0
Dividends	$ 0	$ 0	$ 0	$ 0	$ 0	$ 0	$ 0	$ 0	$ 0	$ 0	$ 0	$ 0
Subtotal Cash Spent	$29,268	$37,069	$38,429	$43,064	$46,161	$50,569	$ 53,393	$ 56,941	$ 57,489	$ 56,960	$ 55,997	$ 49,821
Net Cash Flow	($ 6,268)	($ 11,069)	$ 391	$ 6,197	$18,563	$23,642	$ 33,327	$ 31,316	$ 28,331	$ 25,451	$ 8,003	($ 7,821)
Cash Balance	$33,732	$22,664	$23,055	$29,252	$47,815	$71,457	$104,784	$136,100	$164,431	$189,882	$197,885	$190,064

Table: Balance Sheet

Pro Forma Balance Sheet

Assets	Starting Balances	Month 1	Month 2	Month 3	Month 4	Month 5	Month 6	Month 7	Month 8	Month 9	Month 10	Month 11	Month 12
Current Assets													
Cash	$ 40,000	$ 33,732	$ 22,664	$ 23,055	$ 29,252	$ 47,815	$ 71,457	$ 104,784	$ 136,100	$ 164,431	$ 189,882	$ 197,885	$ 190,064
Accounts Receivable	$ 0	$ 0	$ 0	$ 0	$ 0	$ 0	$ 0	$ 0	$ 0	$ 0	$ 0	$ 0	$ 0
Other Current Assets	$ 0	$ 0	$ 0	$ 0	$ 0	$ 0	$ 0	$ 0	$ 0	$ 0	$ 0	$ 0	$ 0
Total Current Assets	$ 40,000	$ 33,732	$ 22,664	$ 23,055	$ 29,252	$ 47,815	$ 71,457	$ 104,784	$ 136,100	$ 164,431	$ 189,882	$ 197,885	$ 190,064
Long-term Assets													
Long-term Assets	$ 27,000	$ 27,000	$ 27,000	$ 27,000	$ 27,000	$ 27,000	$ 27,000	$ 27,000	$ 27,000	$ 27,000	$ 27,000	$ 27,000	$ 27,000
Accumulated Depreciation	$ 0	$ 142	$ 284	$ 426	$ 568	$ 710	$ 852	$ 994	$ 1,136	$ 1,278	$ 1,420	$ 1,562	$ 1,704
Total Long-term Assets	$ 27,000	$ 26,858	$ 26,716	$ 26,574	$ 26,432	$ 26,290	$ 26,148	$ 26,006	$ 25,864	$ 25,722	$ 25,580	$ 25,438	$ 25,296
Total Assets	$ 67,000	$ 60,590	$ 49,380	$ 49,629	$ 55,684	$ 74,105	$ 97,605	$ 130,790	$ 161,964	$ 190,153	$ 215,462	$ 223,323	$ 215,360

Liabilities and Capital	Month 1	Month 2	Month 3	Month 4	Month 5	Month 6	Month 7	Month 8	Month 9	Month 10	Month 11	Month 12
Current Liabilities												
Accounts Payable	$ 7,760	$ 8,963	$ 13,497	$ 16,445	$ 20,760	$ 23,463	$ 26,991	$ 27,556	$ 27,053	$ 26,295	$ 20,362	$ 13,294
Current Borrowing	$ 0	$ 0	$ 0	$ 0	$ 0	$ 0	$ 0	$ 0	$ 0	$ 0	$ 0	$ 0
Other Current Liabilities	$ 0	$ 0	$ 0	$ 0	$ 0	$ 0	$ 0	$ 0	$ 0	$ 0	$ 0	$ 0
Subtotal Current Liabilities	$ 7,760	$ 8,963	$ 13,497	$ 16,445	$ 20,760	$ 23,463	$ 26,991	$ 27,556	$ 27,053	$ 26,295	$ 20,362	$ 13,294
Long-term Liabilities	$ 0	$ 0	$ 0	$ 0	$ 0	$ 0	$ 0	$ 0	$ 0	$ 0	$ 0	$ 0
Total Liabilities	$ 7,760	$ 8,963	$ 13,497	$ 16,445	$ 20,760	$ 23,463	$ 26,991	$ 27,556	$ 27,053	$ 26,295	$ 20,362	$ 13,294
Paid-in Capital	$130,000	$130,000	$130,000	$130,000	$130,000	$130,000	$130,000	$130,000	$130,000	$130,000	$130,000	$130,000
Retained Earnings	($ 63,000)	($ 63,000)	($ 63,000)	($ 63,000)	($ 63,000)	($ 63,000)	($ 63,000)	($ 63,000)	($ 63,000)	($ 63,000)	($ 63,000)	($ 63,000)
Earnings	($ 14,169)	($ 26,584)	($ 30,868)	($ 27,761)	($ 13,655)	$ 7,142	$ 36,799	$ 67,408	$ 96,100	$ 122,167	$ 135,961	$ 135,066
Total Capital	$ 52,831	$ 40,416	$ 36,132	$ 39,239	$ 53,345	$ 74,142	$ 103,799	$ 134,408	$ 163,100	$ 189,167	$ 202,961	$ 202,066
Total Liabilities and Capital	$ 60,590	$ 49,380	$ 49,629	$ 55,684	$ 74,105	$ 97,605	$ 130,790	$ 161,964	$ 190,153	$ 215,462	$ 223,323	$ 215,360
Net Worth	$ 52,831	$ 40,416	$ 36,132	$ 39,239	$ 53,345	$ 74,142	$ 103,799	$ 134,408	$ 163,100	$ 189,167	$ 202,961	$ 202,066

Net Worth starting balance: $ 67,000

Index